India's External Intelligence

Secrets of Research and Analysis Wing (RAW)

Attention Authors

Manas Publications is fighting a war to tell the world that India can win the battle not only by bullet but also by pen. We are converting fighters into writers since our country is full of intellectuals but their knowledge is only confined to them. No sincere effort has been made by any publisher to give the right direction to their knowledge and the talent of intellectual is still hidden. An author always gives the raw material in the shape of manuscript and it is the sense of publisher to make it a finished product. We are motivating the intellectuals' mind and publishing their manuscripts for more than two decades and would like to publish your manuscript too. If you or your colleagues have any manuscript or are working on, please don't hesitate to contact us with detailed synopsis and contents for its publication. We take utmost care in production and give a wide publicity to the book and its author. We can also suggest you the title for writing related to your subject, since we are the publishers who believe more in quality than in quantity.

India's
External
Intelligence

Secrets of Research and Analysis Wing (RAW)

Major General V.K. Singh

Manas Publications
New Delhi-110002 (INDIA)

Manas Publications

(Publishers, Distributors, Importers & Exporters)
4858, Prahlad Street,
24, Ansari Road, Darya Ganj,
New Delhi - 110 002 (INDIA)
Ph.: 23260783, 23265523:, 23842660 (R)
Fax: 011-23272766
E-mail: manaspublications@vsnl.com
Website: www.manaspublications.com

© Major General V.K. Singh

2007

ISBN 81-7049-332-3
Rs. 495/-

Typeset at
Manas Publications

Printed in India at
Nice Printing Press, Delhi
and Published by Mrs Suman Lata for
Manas Publications, 4858, Prahlad Street,
24, Ansari Road, Darya Ganj,
New Delhi - 110 002 (INDIA)

List of Abbreviations

ALTTC	Advanced Level Telecom Training Centre
ARC	Aviation Research Centre
ASIS	Australian Secret Intelligence Service
ASIO	Australian Security Intelligence Organisation
AT	Acceptance of Tender
ATM	Asynchronous Transfer Mode
ATO	Assistant Technical Officer
BEL	Bharat Electronics Limited.
BJP	Bharatiya Janata Party
BSF	Border Security Force
CAIR	Centre for Artificial Intelligence and Robotics
CALEA	Communication Assistance for Law Enforcement Act (USA)
CAT	Central Administrative Tribunal
C-DOT	Centre for Development of Telematics
CIA	Central Intelligence Agency (USA)
CII	Confederation of Indian Industries
CIS	Counter Intelligence and Security

CGO	Central Government Office
CMIA	Chief Military Intelligence Adviser
CMO	Central Monitoring Organisation
CO	Commanding Officer
COMINT	Communication Intelligence
CSE	Communications Security Establishment (Canada)
CRF	Central Repair Facility
CSD	Canteen Stores Department
CSIS	Canadian Security Intelligence Service
CVC	Central Vigilance Commission
DAMA	Demand Assignment Multiple Access
DFO	Deputy Field Officer
DGMI	Director General Military Intelligence
DGR	Directorate General of Resettlement
DGS	Director General Security
DIA	Defence Intelligence Agency
DIPAC	Defence Image Processing and Analysis Centre
DM	Data Monitoring
DOPT	Department of Personnel and Training
DOT	Department of Telecommunications
DRDO	Defence Research and Development Organisation
DRI	Directorate of Revenue Intelligence
DSD	Defence Security Directorate (Australia)
EOW	Economic Offences Wing
ELINT	Electronic Intelligence
FAT	Factory Acceptance Test

FA	Field Assistant
FBI	Federal Bureau of Investigation (USA)
FIP	Forward Intelligence Post
FO	Field Officer
FOB	Free on Board
GCSB	Government Communications Security Bureau (New Zealand)
GCHQ	Government Communications Headquarters (UK)
GOC	General Officer Commanding
GOC-in-C	General Officer Commanding-in-Chief
HQ	Headquarters
HUMINT	Human Intelligence
IAF	Indian Air Force
IB	Intelligence Bureau
IDS	Integrated Defence Staff
IG, CIA	Inspector General, Central Intelligence Agency
IGIS	Inspector General of Intelligence and Security
ILD	International Long Distance
IISc	Indian Institute of Science
IE	Institute for Engineers
ITE	Institute for Telecommunication Engineers
IMA	Indian Military Academy
IMINT	Imagery Intelligence
IPS	Indian Police Service
ISC	Intelligence and Security Committee
ISI	Inter Services Intelligence (Pakistan)

ISP	Internet Service Provider
ISRO	Indian Space Research Organisation.
ITI	Indian Telephone Industries Limited
ITU	International Telecommunication Union
KGB	*Komitet Gosudarstvennoi Bezopasnosti* (Russian Secret Service)
LC	Letter of Credit
LPDA	Log Periodic Directional Antenna
LTTE	Liberation Force of Tamil Tiger Eelam
MI	Military Intelligence
MI 5	British Secret Service (internal)
MI 6	British Secret Service (external)
MHA	Ministry of Home Affairs
MEA	Ministry of External Affairs
ME/MTech	Master of Engineering/Master of Technology
MOD	Ministry of Defence
MOU	Memorandum of Understanding
MT	Mechanical Transport
NASSCOM	National Association of Software and Service Companies
NCB	Narcotics Control Bureau
NDA	National Defence Academy/National Democratic Alliance
NDC	National Defence College
NTFO	National Technical Facilities Organisation
NTRO	National Technical Resources Organisation
NSC	National Security Council

NSCS	National Security Council Secretariat
NYPD	New York Police Department
NZSIS	New Zealand Security Intelligence Service
OCS	Overseas Communication Service
OFC	Optical Fibre Cable
ORBAT	Order of Battle
OSD	Officer on Special Duty
PA	Personal Assistant
PNC	Price Negotiation Committee
PS	Private Secretary
PMO	Prime Minister's Office
PSU	Public Sector Undertaking
RAS	Research and Analysis Service
RAW	Research and Analysis Wing
RFP	Request for Proposal
RIP	Regulation of Investigation Powers (UK)
SA to RM	Scientific Adviser to the *Raksha Mantri* (Defence Minister),
SAG	System Analysis Group
SB	Special Bureau
SCPC	Single Channel per Carrier
SFO	Senior Field Officer
SIGINT	Signals Intelligence
SIRC	Security Intelligence Review Committee
SSB	Special Services Bureau/Seema Suraksha Bal
SIB	Subsidiary Intelligence Bureau
SFF	Special Frontier Force

SM	Satellite Monitoring
SORM	System of Operative and Investigative Procedures (Russia)
SPG	Special Protection Group
TAC	Tender Acceptance Committee
TAG	Technical Adivsory Group
TDM/TDMA	Time Division Multiplexing/Time Division Multiple Access.
TE	Telecom Equipment
TEC	Technical Evaluation Committee
TECHINT	Technical Intelligence
TM	Terrestrial Monitoring
TO	Technical Officer
UHF	Ultra High Frequency
USAID	United States Agency for International Development
VHF	Very High Frequency
VSAT	Very Small Aperture Terminal
VSNL	Videsh Sanchar Nigam Limited

Preface

The thought of writing a book had not entered my mind until about a year after joining RAW. As time passed, I began to notice several shortcomings and anomalies, which I felt were having a negative impact on the effectiveness of the organisation. Rather than an elite force, which people expected it to be, it had turned into a typical government department, with its attendant ills. Unconsciously, I made comparisons with the Army, where I had spent my entire adult life, and found glaring disparities. The armed forces are also, in a sense, government departments, but are free from most of the ills that plague our bureaucracy. The three services, and each of their components, however small, have a distinct ethos of their own. This *esprit de corps,* as we call it, was totally missing in RAW, which, I thought, was a pity. Unlike other government departments, RAW is not bound by red tape. There are no unions, and officers have extensive powers of punishment as well as reward. There is no shortage of funds, and the organisation has the means not only to increase its efficiency but also improve the quality of life of its members. What, then, was lacking? After a lot of reflection, I thought of two reasons -- lack of leadership and accountability.

Leadership is the key to excellence, in any field, be it the armed forces, education, industry, sports – in fact, almost every human enterprise. If one compares performances of similar entities whose results range from excellent through mediocre to bad, the reasons, in most cases, lie in the performances of leaders, not the members of the groups. During the three and a half years that I spent in RAW, I found several examples of bad leadership, some of which have been included in the book. Of course, it is not to say that all officers of RAW lack leadership. I came across several officers who would do credit to any organisation, and these stood out in the crowd. In fact, were it not for these officers, RAW would not have enjoyed the reputation and standing it still has in the intelligence community. Unfortunately, they were in a minority.

Having worked for almost ten years on a book about military leaders, I could not help draw inferences regarding the presence or absence of this quality from everyday events that happened around me. This was the first time I had to work with people who often did not mean what they said. In the Army, one dealt with colleagues – and that includes superiors and subordinates – with all cards on the table. No one had a hidden agenda, or an axe to grind. If a soldier appeared to be extra dutiful or deferential, all that he probably wanted was a few days leave. And when a colleague turned on the charm, he had nothing more sinister in mind than borrowing your golf clubs. Mistakes were acknowledged and rebukes accepted, with no hard feelings on either side. But here in RAW, things were different. The mutual trust and concern for each other that we had taken for granted while in uniform were missing. As a result, one always felt a little uneasy when interacting with others, which is obviously not the best way to get things done.

More than leadership and trust, the most glaring shortcoming seemed to be lack of accountability. Since RAW was not answerable to any outside agency – the control of the PMO was perfunctory, at best – many officers thought that they were not only above the law but a law unto themselves. This sort of belief is often found in police and intelligence agencies in totalitarian regimes, but appear out of place in a democracy, such as ours. This superciliousness and arrogance often translated into activities that could not be termed as lawful or honourable. Unlike in other developed societies such as the USA, where the legislature acts a watchdog on every organ of the executive, including intelligence and security agencies, in India these organisations were beyond the pale of parliamentary review. Their actions, however improper, would never be brought to the notice of the public. This appeared to me an unacceptable state of affairs, totally against the democratic principles that are enshrined in our Constitution

I tried to find out what other people had written about RAW. Apart from a book by Ashok Raina, which was published in 1981, very few Indian authors have attempted to write on the subject. Of course, articles have appeared from time to time, but since most of these have been written by people who have never served in RAW, they are often speculative and inaccurate. An exception is B. Raman, an ex- Additional Secretary of RAW, who writes regularly in journals and newspapers. Strangely enough, several books have been written on RAW in Pakistan, including some by scholars who have undertaken research projects funded by the government or professional institutions. But most of the writing is biased and imprecise, which is not surprising, given the history of bad blood between the two nations since Independence.

Writing about an intelligence agency in India is no easy task. For one, there is very little information in the public domain. Ironically, we know more about the CIA than about RAW, because everything about the former is on their official website. The Right to Information Act has been passed, but the intelligence agencies are beyond its purview. The Official Secrets Act, 1923, was a draconian law passed during British rule, to be used against Indians who were found to be acting against British imperialist interests. Though totally out of date, the law has not been repealed, in spite of vociferous demands from many quarters. With the enactment of the Right to

Information Act, the Official Secrets Act has become an anachronism that deserves to be consigned to oblivion. One of the most violated provisions of the Act relates to contact with foreigners. According to the Act, Government officials cannot meet, converse or have any contact with foreign nationals without obtaining permission from their departments. I wonder how many officers who are regularly seen with foreign diplomats at Page 3 parties follow these rules.

There is little doubt that the concept of security has changed during the eighty years since the Official Secrets Act was promulgated, especially after Independence. With the resources available today, very little can be hidden. Until very recently, it was forbidden to take photographs even of railway bridges. With satellite imagery, even much smaller objects can be pinpointed in far greater detail than any photograph taken by a conventional camera. Similarly, the strength and dispositions of military units was considered a highly classified subject. Today, the complete ORBAT (Order of Battle) is known to everyone, including the opposite side. Information concerning aircraft, ships, tanks and similar armaments that was heavily guarded is now available on the Internet. Publications such as Jane's regularly give out details of the military inventory of every country. The only thing classified today is the mind of the commander i.e. the way he is going to fight the battle.

Though I had more or less decided to write this book before I left RAW, what strengthened my resolve was the publication of Maloy Dhar's book on the IB, called *Open Secrets*. Around this time, I also came across Brigadier Tirmazi's book about the ISI, called *Profiles of Intelligence*. Both Dhar and Tirmazi have given details of operations conducted by these agencies, in which they were involved. In this book, I have not included any operation of RAW for the simple reason that I was never involved in any. My job involved communications and signals intelligence, and I have primarily dealt with these subjects. Even here, only a few case studies have been included, to bring out some aberrations.

What then is the reason for writing this book? I feel that the Indian taxpayer has a right to know how public money is spent. He may not be interested in details, but he would certainly want an assurance that it is not being squandered, or put to illegitimate use. There is a need to bring all organs of the state under the supervision of Parliament, without exception. If the defence forces can be subject to statutory audit and parliamentary review, I do not see any reason why intelligence agencies should be exempted. Members of Parliament are public servants, and keeping information from them is an affront to their integrity and loyalty to the country.

Major General VK Singh
New Delhi

Contents

1

From Soldier to Spy

After spending 35 years in uniform - 39, if one were to count the years spent in the NDA and IMA – I joined the, Cabinet Secretariat, Research and Analysis Wing (RAW) in November 2000. I was at that time posted as the Chief Signal Officer, Western Command, at Chandimandir, near Chandigarh. The decision to make the transition from career soldier to professional spy may appear strange, especially at the fag end of one's career. However, I made the switch not because of any expertise or experience – I had never served in an appointment dealing with intelligence – but purely on grounds of career advancement, or rather, extension. The retirement age for major generals was 58, and I was due to retire in June 2002. (In fact, it had been 56, just three years earlier, and I would have retired in 2000, had it not been raised by two years). Being from the Corps of Signals, I was eligible for only two appointments in the rank of lieutenant general, for which the retirement age was 60. One was the Signal Officer-in-Chief, based in Delhi, and the other was the Commandant, Military College of Telecommunication Engineering, based in Mhow. Both appointments were held by officers who were due to retire after June 2002. This meant that my selection board for promotion from major general to lieutenant general would either not be held before I retired, or even if it was, and I was approved, I would still have to retire, due to lack of a vacancy. In such cases, the best option was to side step to a civil government appointment, where the retirement age was 60, irrespective of rank.

Sometime in the middle of the year 2000, Army Headquarters asked for volunteers in the rank of major general from Signals for deputation to RAW. The appointments, in the rank of Joint Secretary, were temporary, under a project known as Vision 2000. The deputation was for a period of three years or till the date of retirement, whichever was earlier. Several other officers from the Armed Forces had earlier gone on deputation to RAW, and informal enquiries revealed that after retirement from the respective service, they were usually re-employed in the same appointment, up to the age of 60. Along with a few of my colleagues, I volunteered. After several months, we were called for an interview. This was my first introduction to the organization, about which I had heard and read a lot, but knew very little.

I was asked to report for the interview at the main gate of the building, which houses the headquarters of RAW in Delhi. When I asked for the address, I was told that it was in the CGO Complex, near the Nehru Stadium. When I asked if there was a signboard in front of the building, I was told that there was none. Then how would I know where to go, I asked? I was advised that I should come through the complex that housed the headquarters of the Border Security Force or the Central Reserve Police Force, which were located next door, and ask for directions. In fact, as it turned out, I need not have worried. Any taxi or auto driver, or the dozens of vendors who sell eatables outside the CGO Complex will gladly guide you to the correct location. I was reminded of the time I was in the Soviet Union in 1987, when the KGB buildings in Moscow and Leningrad were unmarked, but all Russians knew about them, whispering *'bolshoi dom'* (big

.I was told to reach the gate about 30 minutes before the appointed hour, where someone would meet me. Since I was in uniform, and alighted from my staff car that had two stars and a flag, the 'someone' had no difficulty in spotting me. He already had a pass made out for me and led me to the building, where there was another Reception, where my details were recorded in a register. I was then led to a room on the eleventh floor, where I found four other persons waiting for the interview. Two of them were my colleagues from the Army, while the other two were civilians. Most of them seemed to be better informed than I was about the organization and the interview panel. I learned that there were two vacancies, out of which one was likely to be filled by an Army officer and the other by a civilian. The interview panel comprised the Special Secretary (S), Mr. Sunder Rajan, the Additional Secretary (Personnel), Mr. RK Shanmugam, and the Additional Secretary (Telecom), Dr. VK Singh.

The interview went off without a hitch, with some innocuous questions regarding my career and experience. In any case, they had already obtained our dossiers from the Military Secretary's Branch in Army HQ, and had probably gone through my annual confidential reports. It was only after the interview was over that Shanmugam asked me which squadron I had been while undergoing training in the NDA. When I said 'Bravo', he asked me if I remembered him. When I replied in the negative he asked, "Who was the SCC of 23rd Course?" It was only then that it dawned on me that I had failed to recognize him. When he was in the NDA, his name had been R. Kumar, and the surname was not used. But I should have recognized his face even if it was 37 years since we last met. I could do little more than apologise, but Shanmugam only smiled and said, "Obviously, I did not give you enough front rolls."

A few days after my return to Chandimandir, I was telephonically informed that I had been selected. It was another three months before I received the posting orders, asking me to join at the earliest. I thought Army HQ would post a suitable officer to relieve me, but it did not happen and I had to move without relief. The Kargil operations had taken place just a year earlier, and there were a number of telecommunication projects that I was handling at that time. As is well known, the Western Command is the most important in the Indian Army, having the bulk of its strike capability, and keeping it without a Chief Signal Officer was perhaps not the most prudent of decisions. Naturally, HQ Western Command protested, but was overruled by Army HQ, who clarified that the appointment I was going to fill was 'critical', and I was to be relieved immediately. As I found later, this was nothing but fiction – for almost a month after I reported, I did not even have an office, let alone any work being assigned to me. This was typical of the difference in the functioning of the Army and the civil bureaucracy. All that I could do was to leave detailed handing/taking over notes for my successor. After the usual round of farewells I handed over charge to my deputy and left for Delhi, reporting to my new appointment on 10 November 2000.

The first person I met was Brigadier Subhas Datta, from Signals, who was then posted in the Telecom Division as Director (TE). He was from the 1962 batch, and senior to me by three years. Being from the same regiment i.e. Signals, we had been meeting off and on and I had known him for well nigh forty years. In fact, he was the one who had given me most of the 'gen' about RAW before I joined. Needless to say, he was of great help even afterwards, right up to the time he left the organization on superannuation. Apart from Datta, there were two other Signals officers in RAW at that time. Brigadier RC Manchanda (63 batch) was then posted as Additional Commissioner in Jodhpur, while Brigadier Ujjal Dasgupta (66 batch), or UD as we called him, was the Director (Computers). Of course, there were several other officers from the Army, most of them from the Armoured Corps or Infantry. The only other officer of my rank was Major General PK Puri, who was the CMIA (Chief Military Intelligence Adviser). He had under him several officers from the Army, Navy and Air Force. Prem Puri was from the same batch as Subhas Datta, and the two were good friends. In addition to these officers, who were on deputation or re-employed, there were many others who had joined RAW in the early years as majors or captains. They had been absorbed in RAW, and did not use their ranks. The seniormost among them were RK Shanmugam and RS Bedi (63 batch).

Datta took me along to PK Mathur, the Deputy Secretary (Pers), who gave me several forms to fill. I spent the day in Datta's office, filling forms and generally getting acquainted with others who visited his office. The next day, I met the Joint Secretary (Security), UK Katna, who gave me a book containing the instructions on security. He advised me to read it at my leisure, and return it after I had done with it. I also met the Additional Secretary (Telecom), Dr. VK Singh, who was to be my immediate superior. For some reason, he was also known as Adviser (Telecom). Apart from me, there were two other joint secretaries in the Telecom Division. One of them was RL Verma, who was from the permanent telecom cadre of RAW. The other joint secretary was VS Yadav, who had joined along with me, on deputation from ISRO (Indian Space Research Organisation).

During my first week, I called upon the senior officers then serving in RAW. The Director, RAW and Secretary (R) was AS Dulat, who was to retire in another three months time. He was from the IB (Intelligence Bureau), the traditional rivals of RAW. The head of RAW in fact wore two hats, having line and staff functions. As Director, RAW, he was head of the organization, with line or command responsibilities. He was also a secretary to the Government of India, with the designation Secretary (R). In the latter appointment, he was assisted by a special secretary, known as Special Secretary (SR), who had his office in Bikaner House, on Shah Jahan Road. This was also the official address of RAW, used in all letters going out, and where all incoming mail was delivered. The Special Secretary (SR) at that time was Y Hari Shankar, who had earlier been the Director General of Police of Haryana. The ARC (Aviation Research Centre), located in a neighbouring building, was an independent organization headed by a Director of the rank of special secretary, who reported to the Director RAW. The Director ARC was RS Bedi, an ex-Cavalry officer. The Special Frontier Force, (SFF) headed by an Inspector General, functioned under the ARC. The IG SFF was Major General Bhopinder Singh, who was from my course at the NDA and IMA.

Under the Secretary, there were two special secretaries, Sunder Rajan and Vikram Sood. Sunder Rajan was the senior of the two, and tipped to be the next Secretary. He was feared due to his acerbic and brusque style, which was in contrast to Sood's suave and mild manner. Their designations were not fixed, and varied from the first letters of their names to the areas of responsibility, i.e. East or West. There were two additional secretaries – CD Sahay and JK Sinha - with operational responsibilities. In addition, there was an additional secretary (Shanmugam) looking after personnel and administration, while another (Dr. VK Singh) headed the Telecom Division, of which I was to be a part.

After having met the senior officers, I thought I should go and meet the joint secretaries. However, there were too many of them, and I was told that it was not necessary, since I would never have much to do with most of them during the course of my duties. The Annual Conference was to be held after a month or so, and I would be able to meet most of them at that time. In fact, there were some directors whom I did not get to meet until almost a year later, when I began to attend the weekly conference on Thursday. RL Verma used to attend the weekly conference, but both Yadav and I were not invited, as someone felt that it was not necessary. This was an indication of the lowly status of the Telecom Division in RAW, of which I was to find further evidence as time passed. This was in stark contrast to the Army, where the Signals officer is part of the Commander's 'O' Group or inner circle, and nothing is done without consulting him. I had a premonition that I was not going to like the new outfit that I had joined.

2

A Brief History

There is no official document that gives out the history of RAW. Neither is it possible to get an accurate picture of its evolution, organisation and present status. Unlike the Army, RAW does not maintain a Digest of Service or War Diary, which can serve as a historical record of its activities. A number of books have been written, by Indian and Pakistani authors, giving out the history of RAW and its activities. A large number of articles have appeared in journals and newspapers, from time to time. However, almost all of them are inaccurate, based on conjecture and guesswork rather than accurate data or reliable information. To cite an example, the organisation of RAW in 1968 has been given by Ashok Raina in his book on RAW, published in 1981.[1] This has been reproduced in Fahmida Ashraf's book published by the Institute of Strategic Studies, Islamabad, in 2004, which also gives the current organizational structure of RAW. Without going into details, I would only say that both are not entirely accurate. The Pakistani book has many other gaffes – according to them the Central Monitoring Organisation is part of the Signals Intelligence Directorate of the Army, the ARC is under the Ministry of Defence, and the Joint Cipher Bureau is responsible for SIGINT.[2]

In most democratic nations, intelligence agencies are under the executive control of the elected government but are finally accountable to the legislature, which in most cases, approves not only their funding and but also their charter. Though RAW is modelled on the CIA of USA and Mossad of Israel, its detailed organisation, size and funding is not known to Parliament. Significantly, the organisational structure of both CIA and Mossad are in the public domain, and available in various publications as well as on the Internet. This lack of parliamentary supervision and accountability has probably done more harm than good to the country, a fact that has been commented by several experts. Without a specific objective, clear priorities and unambiguous channels of tasking, RAW has often been accused of tilting at windmills. A case in point was the failure of the agency to detect the intrusions in Kargil in 1999. The Kargil Review Committee, headed by K Subramanyam, found that surveillance aircraft of the ARC (Aviation Research Centre), which functions under RAW, had been concentrating on Tibet instead of Kargil!

Intelligence Services in India have their origins in the British Raj. In 1885, Major General Sir Charles Metcalfe MacGregor was appointed Quartermaster General and head of the Intelligence Department of the British Indian Army. The objective then was to monitor Russian troop deployments in Afghanistan, fearing a Russian invasion of British India through Central Asia. Russia had strong imperial ambitions and a special interest in South Asia. Before General MacGregor's appointment, an organization called the Survey of India, located in Dehradun, performed the basic intelligence functions. It gathered topographical information and made maps based on the information provided by its agents on the borders. In 1921, a new state-run surveillance and monitoring agency — Indian Political Intelligence (IPI) - was established. The IPI was run jointly by the India Office and the Government of India and reported jointly to the Secretary of the Public and Judicial Department of the India Office, and the Director of Intelligence

Bureau (DIB) in India, and maintained close contact with Scotland Yard and MI5. In 1947, it was reorganized as the Central Intelligence Bureau under the Ministry of Home Affairs.

Soon after Independence, the IB (Intelligence Bureau) was set up, with Sanjivi Pillai as its first Director. After Mahatma Gandhi's assassination in 1948, Sanjivi was replaced by BN Mullick, who remained the head of the organisation for an unprecedented 17 years. During his tenure, the IB became an extremely powerful organization, looking after external as well as internal intelligence, in addition to playing a major role in deciding foreign policy. Mullick's proximity to Nehru added to his clout, and during the 1962 conflict with China, he even decided the location of border outposts manned by the Army, with predictable results. Mullick had a part to play in another unsavoury incident, which almost ended the career of a bright Army officer. In 1961, at the behest of Lieutenant General BM Kaul, Mullick produced an intelligence report about the anti national views of Major General SHFJ Manekshaw, the Commandant of the Staff College in Wellington. Mullick refused to appear before the Court of Inquiry that was ordered against Manekshaw, who was later cleared of all charges. After the 1962 debacle, Sam took over command of 4 Corps from Kaul, who resigned in disgrace. [3]

Sanjivi had tried to set up a foreign intelligence unit within the IB, and obtained the approval of the government to post officers in the Indian embassies in Germany, France and Pakistan. Subsequently, IB officers were posted to several other countries, such as China, Burma, Sri Lanka and the Middle East region. However, the genesis of the decision to create RAW lay in the 1962 conflict, when our intelligence failed to detect Chinese build up for the attack. Brigadier MN Batra, the DMI (Director of Military Intelligence) at that time, recalls that he had to face a lot of flak on this account and had quite a job explaining to everyone that responsibility for strategic military intelligence across the border lay with the IB and not MI. Batra argued that there was an urgent need for an external intelligence agency and convinced the Army Chief, General JN Choudhury, who pursued it with vigour. Accompanied by Batra, Choudhury visited the USA and UK to see the functioning of their foreign intelligence agencies. On their return Batra was asked to write a paper on the subject. (MN Batra was the DMI for 10 years, from 1961 to 1971 and retired as a lieutenant general. When he was the DMI, his cousin, Major General RN Batra was the Director of Signals and Signal Officer-in-Chief. Both of them set up the Signals Intelligence Directorate, at about the same time. RN Batra, who also retired as a lieutenant general, is credited with laying the foundations of modern communications in the Indian Army).

MN Batra's paper, which proposed the establishment of a foreign intelligence agency was put up to the Defence Minister, YB Chavan. Indira Gandhi, who had become Prime Minister after the sudden demise of Lal Bahadur Shastri in Tashkent in 1965, approved the creation of the agency but unlike the CIA and MI6, decided to keep it under her own control instead of the Ministry of Defence. The new organization, known as the Research & Analysis Wing of the Cabinet Secretariat, was established on 21 September 1968. Rameshwar Nath Kao was selected to be the first head of the RAW, with K. Sankaran Nair as his deputy. Kao and Nair were both from the IB, and had earlier helped in establishing the foreign intelligence set up in Ghana, where Prime Minister Nehru had sent them in response to a request from President Kwame Nkrumah.[4]

Apart from Kao and Sankaran, about 250 personnel moved to RAW from IB, which provided most of the manpower for the new organization during its initial years. In effect, the IB was bifurcated, and many IB officers continued to be part of both organizations. Even during the 1971 operations against East Pakistan, the IB's Joint Director in Calcutta, PN Bannerji, was also the RAW Commissioner. In 1971, Kao persuaded the government to set up the Aviation Research Centre (ARC) with the assistance of the USA to carry out aerial reconnaissance. Having started with 250 personnel and an annual budget of Rs 2 crore (by a rough estimate), by the early seventies the annual budget of RAW had risen to Rs 30 crores while its personnel numbered several thousand. In 1976, Kao was promoted to the rank of a Secretary responsible for Security, reporting directly to the Prime Minister. To a large extent, it was Kao who raised RAW to the level of India's premier intelligence agency, with agents in virtually every major embassy and high commission.

RAW suffered a serious setback when the Janata government led by Morarji Desai came to power in 1977, with Atal Behari Vajpeyi as the external affairs minister. Having experienced the excesses during the Emergency, they were distrustful of the functioning of RAW, and the loyalty of its officers. Morarji Desai ordered a review of the functioning of the organization and severe cuts in its size and expenditure. K Sankaran Nair, who had succeeded RN Kao as the Director only three months earlier, resigned in protest. After Indira Gandhi returned to power, she got him back, with a mandate to restructure the organization and streamline it's functioning.

During the 80s and the 90s RAW continued to increase in size and expand its coverage. Though it earned kudos for its successes in Bangladesh, it came in for severe criticism for its role in supporting the LTTE in Sri Lanka, which backfired, leading to the induction of Indian troops in the Island. From its very inception, RAW has focused its attention on Pakistan and China, the two countries with whom India has fought major wars after Independence. Not surprisingly, more has been written about RAW in Pakistan than in India. Pakistan has blamed India for many acts of sabotage, terrorism and political events, including the creation of Bangladesh. According to published sources in Pakistan, RAW has an extensive network of agents working in Pakistan, in collaboration with sectarian and ethnic groups in Sindh and Punjab. Quoting an unknown and probably fictitious American group called the Federation of American Scientists (FAS),

Pakistani sources claim that as many as 35,000 RAW agents have penetrated Pakistan between 1983-93, and about 40 terrorist training camps were being run in Rajasthan, Punjab, Kashmir and UP by the Special Service Bureau (SSB). They also blame RAW for the hijacking of the Indian Airlines plane to Lahore in 1971, in order to bequeath a terrorist label to the Kashmiri separatist movement. Another startling claim is that RAW agents located in the USA intercept long distance telephone calls! Of course, all these allegations are unsubstantiated, and give more credit to RAW than it deserves.[5]

One Pakistani author who has written extensively on RAW is Group Captain SM Hali, who has not only given a detailed account of its activities but also listed the major successes and failures of RAW. According to him, the major 'successes' of RAW were the creation of Bangladesh; the assassination of General Zia-ur-Rahman; Project Poornima (Pokharan nuclear explosion); the Kahuta Blueprint (the Indians were on the verge of obtaining it, but Morarji Desai refused to sanction the $ 10,000 demanded by the RAW agent, and informed Pakistan, who caught and eliminated the RAW mole); induction of Sikkim into the Indian Union; engineering a revolt in the Maldives (to increase India's influence); Operation Chanakya (engineering atrocities on Kashmiri Pandits in Kashmir); and monitoring Pakistani telecommunications. Among RAW's 'failures' are the promulgation of Emergency (Kao supported it, whereas the IB had advised against it); Operation Blue Star (RAW failed to assess the strength of Bhindranwale's forces); Mujib-ur-Rahman's assassination (RAW had advance information about Mujib's assassination but failed to prevent it); defeat of Sir Seewoosagur Ramgoolam in Mauritius elections (Indira Gandhi wanted him to win); support to LTTE, which later turned against it; and blowing up Air India Flight 182 to Canada in 1985 in order to malign the Sikhs. Again, some of the assertions are not only outrageous, but downright laughable. If RAW failed to acquire the Kahuta blueprint, and Pakistan eliminated the mole, how can it be termed a success? The same applies to the alleged atrocities on Kashmiri Pandits. It has not helped India, so how can it be termed a success for RAW? These operations may have been a success for the ISI, but certainly not for RAW. [6]

The hijacking of the Indian Airlines aircraft from Kathmandu in December 1999 created headlines and remained in the news for several weeks. One question that has still not been answered is why no attempt was made to storm the aircraft when it was at Amritsar. The then Minister for External Affairs, Jaswant Singh, has described the incident in his recently published book, *A Call to Honour.* According to him, he had given clear orders that the aircraft should not be allowed to take off from Amritsar. Yet it took off, and landed in Kandahar. Subsequently three dreaded terrorists – Maulana Masood Azhar, then a top leader of the Harkat-ul-Mujahideen; Omar Sheikh, a British national who was a devoted follower of Maulana Masood Azhar; and Mushtaq Ahmed Zargar, the chief commander of the Al-Umar Mujhahideen, - were set free. Reportedly a large sum of money was also paid for the release of the 155 passengers and crew of the aircraft. This was done in spite of a decision of the Cabinet that there will be no negotiation with these hijackers. Why did this happen? Fahmida Ashraf , a senior research fellow at the Institute of Strategic Studies, Islamabad has an answer. Quoting a report in the *Asiaweek* issue of January 21, 2000 , she asserts that the real reason for not ordering the attack on the aircraft at Amritsar was that the brother-in-law of NK Singh, the senior-most bureaucrat in India's Prime Minister's Office was on the plane. 'The report identified him a Shashi Bhushan Singh, a senior police officer assigned to India's premier counterintelligence organization, the Research and Analysis Wing (RAW), and who was working apparently under cover – in the Indian embassy in Kathmandu, where the hijackers initially boarded the plane on December 24[7]. The story may or may not be true, but it brings out the clout which RAW supposedly enjoys, especially in Pakistan. It also throws some light on the authority wielded by the PMO and the bureaucrats serving in that office.

In 1999 RAW came in for severe criticism for its failure to detect the infiltration of a large number of Pakistani troops in the Kargil sector, which necessitated a major operation by the Indian Army, resulting in heavy casualties. The Government constituted a committee to go into the reasons for the intelligence failure, and recommend remedial measures. The Kargil Review Committee, as it came to be called, was headed by K Subrahmanyam, a former Director of the IDSA (Institute of Defence Studies and Analysis), and one of India's most respected defence analysts. The other members of the committee were B G Verghese, a well known journalist; Lieutenant General K K Hazari a retired Vice Chief of the Army; and Satish Chandra, Chairman of the JIC (Joint Intelligence Committee).

The committee pointed out several lacunae in the existing intelligence set up in the country, the chief being the existence of multiple agencies reporting to different heads. It decried the virtual monopoly of RAW in respect of external intelligence, and commented adversely on the wisdom of saddling one agency alone with multifarious responsibilities of human, communication, imagery and electronic intelligence. It recommended that all COMINT (Communication Intelligence) and ELINT (Electronic Intelligence) efforts be grouped under a single organisation like the NSA (National Security Agency) of the USA, which is under the DOD (Department of Defence). In the UK, GCHQ (Government Communication Head Quarters) controlling TECHINT (Technical Intelligence) is under the MOD (Ministry of Defence). The committee felt that the resources of Signals Intelligence Directorate and DIPAC (Defence Image Processing and Analysis Centre) supplemented by all other national resources of COMINT, ELINT, IMINT and TECHINT (including space reconnaissance) need to be grouped under one agency, which could be called the DIA (Defence

Intelligence Agency). This would avoid duplication and result in optimal utilisation of national assets of strategic importance.

The recommendations of the Kargil Review Committee were examined by the Group of Ministers (GoM) established in April 2000. Prime Minister Atal Behari Vajpayee chaired the GoM, the other key members being Defence Minister George Fernandes, External Affairs Minister Jaswant Singh and Finance Minister Yashwant Sinha. The GoM decided to constitute four task forces, which were to study intelligence, defence management, internal security and border management respectively, and examine the critical appreciation of India's security establishment by the Kargil Review Committee Report. The task force on intelligence was to be chaired by Jammu and Kashmir Governor Girish Chandra Saxena, who had headed RAW in 1983-86. The other members of the task force were former Foreign Secretary K Raghunath, former IB chief MK Narayanan, former Special Secretary, Home, PP Shrivastava, former RAW Additional Secretary B Raman, and R Narsimha of the National Institute of Advanced Studies.

In February 2001, Union Home Minister LK Advani announced that the government had accepted the findings of the task forces. The meticulously researched report of the task force on intelligence was the most significant of the four, calling on India's intelligence establishment to take "an honest and in-depth stock of their present intelligence effort and capabilities to meet challenges and problems". It recommended wide ranging upgradation of signals, electronics, imaging, economic intelligence and counter-intelligence capabilities, in addition to systemic changes in conventional intelligence gathering. RAW was to be restructured, making it a leaner organisation, divested of redundant organisations such as the Seema Suraksha Bal (SSB), which had originally been raised as a paramilitary force along the border with China. Most of the 30,000 personnel of the SSB would be inducted in the Indo-Tibetan Border Police (ITBP), with a few being transferred to the IB. RAW was permitted to retain the Aviation Research Centre (ARC), which the Army had demanded be given to it, in order to prevent fiascos like the Kargil intrusions. However, it agreed to give the Army more direct representation and involvement in day-to-day operations of the ARC.

The government agreed to the creation of a Defence Intelligence Agency (DIA), whose head would be the adviser to the Chief of Staffs Committee and the Defence Minister. The DIA chief would also control two of the military intelligence establishment's most powerful institutions, the Signals Intelligence Directorate and the Defence Image Processing and Analysis Centre (DIPAC). The DIA will be empowered to conduct transborder operations. This is in fact only a formalization of the power already given to Military Intelligence for such operations. It is understood that Prime Minister VP Singh granted a secret authorisation in 1990-1991 to Military Intelligence to conduct tactical intelligence operations to a limited distance across the border. The DIA will now be able to conduct operations for tactical intelligence coverage in all of Pakistan. Similar powers to carry out trans-border operations have been given to the IB. However, the primacy of RAW in external intelligence was left untouched.

An important recommendation of the GoM was a formal charter for the IB and RAW. Strangely enough, both agencies did not have a written charter, and had been functioning in accordance with the wishes and whims of the political leadership, or in most cases, their own judgment. The IB's charter included the responsibility for the collection and dissemination of all intelligence on internal security, making it the nodal organisation for counter-terrorist and counter-intelligence work. It was also made responsible for ensuring the security of information systems and would have an independent COMINT capability.

When RAW came into being in 1968, it was not given a formal charter, though Raina has listed some objectives of RAW in the field of operations. Since that time, RAW had made several requests for its role and responsibilities being clearly defined so that there is no overlap in respect of external intelligence with other agencies. Though no formal charter was issued, in 1990 the Prime Minister approved the basic tasks that RAW was expected to carry out. The GoM felt that along with the IB, a formal charter should also be given to RAW, so that there is no ambiguity regarding its role. The GoM recommended the following charter for RAW: -

- Collection, production, analysis and assessment of all forms of external intelligence of interest to India, in political, military, economic, scientific and technological fields, as well as its timely dissemination to all concerned organisations/agencies.

- Conducting special operations abroad, including psychological warfare. Other agencies could carry out such tasks, after clearance of the Prime Minister, in consultation and coordination with RAW. However, the DIA could conduct HUMINT operations for tactical related defence intelligence, after obtaining government approval.

- Act as nodal agency for counter intelligence operations outside India.

- Liaison with foreign intelligence and security agencies in India and abroad. However, the IB could be permitted to liaise with foreign agencies in matters concerning counter-terrorism after government approval and in consultation and coordination with RAW.

- RAW is an integral part of the Cabinet Secretariat and will report to the Prime Minister.

- RAW would work in close coordination with the Ministry of External Affairs. On intelligence matters, Secretary (R) could report, at his discretion, to the Ministers of External Affairs, Home and Finance.

The recommendations of the GoM have by and large been implemented. It has resulted in several new organisations being raised and the charters of the existing ones defined. However, this has not removed the anomalies and lacunae that existed earlier, especially relating to the overlap between the activities of the intelligence agencies. Earlier, RAW was the only organisation permitted to conduct espionage operations abroad. Now both IB and DIA have been given the authority to conduct such operations, with government approval. The technical intelligence capability of IB, which had been severely curtailed after the creation of RAW, has largely been restored. IB now has independent communications intelligence capability, which would enable it to monitor all forms of cellular, landline, radio and Internet traffic. It will have its own cryptographic resources, along with state-of-the-art direction-finding equipment to locate transmissions, including those by terrorists in areas like Jammu and Kashmir.[8]

Another new organisation that was created by the government is the National Technical Facilities Organisation (NTFO), which was subsequently renamed the National Technical Research Organisation (NTRO). This is modeled on the lines of the National Security Agency (NSA) in the USA, which controls all technical intelligence collection resources. However, there are differences between the two both with regard to their charter as well as the chain of command. The (NSA) has two principal missions: designing cipher systems that will protect the integrity of US information systems and searching for weaknesses in adversaries' systems and codes. It coordinates, directs, and performs highly specialised activities to protect US information systems and produce foreign intelligence information. It is a high technology organisation, which is on the frontiers of communication and data processing. All the COMINT and SIGINT efforts of the USA are grouped under one single organisation of NSA, which is one of several elements of the intelligence community administered by the Department of Defence (DOD).[9]

In contrast, the NTRO in India will not have exclusive control over such resources. Several other agencies such as RAW, IB and DIA will continue to maintain their COMINT and SIGINT assets. The NTRO's attempts to get the IMINT resources from ARC were stonewalled by RAW, in spite of the fact that the first head of NTRO, RS Bedi, was an ex-RAW officer who was earlier heading the ARC. As a result, NTRO will have to procure its own aircraft with IMINT capabilities, another instance of duplication of scarce resources and wasteful expenditure.

The DIA of USA is also different from the DIA in India. In the USA, the DIA, which came into being in October 1961, is the primary producer of foreign military intelligence, in contrast to the Indian intelligence system. It fulfils a critically important need for a central intelligence manager for DOD to support the requirements of the Secretary of Defence, the Joint Chiefs of Staff (JCS), and the military forces, as well as other policy makers. Prior to the creation of DIA, respective military departments separately collected, produced and disseminated intelligence for their individual use, just as is still being done in India. The creation of the DIA under the DOD removed most of the flaws noticed in the earlier intelligence set-up in the USA. A similar reorganization was forced upon British Military Intelligence in 1964 with the creation of single unified Defence Staff. The former Admiralty, the War Office and Air Ministry were abolished and merged into Ministry of Defence (MOD), the separate departments then became known as MOD (Navy), MOD (Army) and MOD (RAF). Their intelligence organisations were also merged along with Joint Intelligence Board (which was responsible for obtaining scientific and TECHINT) to form the Defence Intelligence Staff.[10]

RAW has undergone many changes in its brief history of 39 years since it was raised. Though its present organisation, size and funding remain a closely guarded secret, its activities are often highlighted in the Press. From a once faceless organisation it is slowly emerging from the shadows. Until a few years ago, one never saw a photograph of the RAW chief in a newspaper. With the recent practice of the heads of RAW and IB standing in line to see off the Prime Minister before his foreign visits, one can see them not only in the newspapers but also on TV news channels. Today, RAW is counted among the premier intelligence agencies of the world. However, the problems of ad hoc-ism and lack of cohesion remain. Most important, it has not been able to develop a distinct ethos of its own.

End Notes:

1. Ashok Raina, *Inside RAW: The Story of India's Secret Service*, p.1

2. Fahmida Ashraf, *RAW: Covert Instrument of Indian Ambitions*, pp.50-51.

3. Major General V.K. Singh, *Leadership in the Indian Army: Biographies of Twelve Soldiers*, p.197

4. Ashok Raina, pp.13-14.

5. Aslam Khan, 'US report details direct RAW involvement in East Pakistan secession', *Pakistan Defence Journal*, February 2000.

6. Group Captain SM Hali,. 'RAW at War-Genesis of Secret Agencies in Ancient India', *Pakistan Defence Journal*, March 1999.

7. Fahmida Ashraf, p.33

8. Praveen Swami, 'For a paradigm shift', *Frontline*, 13 April, 2001.

9. Vinod Anand, 'An Integrated And Joint Approach Towards Defence Intelligence', *IDSA Journal*, November 2000, (Vol. XXIV No. 8).

10. Vinod Anand, quoting Peter Gudgin, *Military Intelligence: The British Story* (London: Arms and Armour Press, 1989), p. 75

3

Learning the Ropes

Within a month of my joining, the annual conference was held. This was attended by all heads of station within the country, as well as in neighbouring countries. The conference lasted three days, and gave me an opportunity to meet most of the officers of the organization. Of course, there were many more serving abroad in various countries, whom I would probably never meet. The conference also helped me to get a clearer picture of the manner in which the organization functioned. This was the last conference chaired by Mr. Dulat, who retired soon afterwards, moving to the Prime Minister's Office as an OSD (Officer on Special Duty), looking after Kashmir affairs. Vikram Sood was appointed the next 'Chief', probably in the interest of continuity. (RAW has adopted the MI-6 practice of referring to the Director as 'Chief'). Sunder Rajan, though senior, had very little residual service, and lost out in the race. He too moved out of RAW, being appointed an OSD. Before joining RAW, Sood had been in the Postal Department, and was sometimes facetiously referred to as the 'dak wallah'. At that time, most of the senior positions in RAW as well as IB were occupied by officers from the IPS (Indian Police Service), who felt that all others were outsiders.

Bit by bit, I began to learn about the organization that I had joined. Of course, I had known that it looked after external intelligence, while the IB looked after internal intelligence. The responsibilities of the two often overlapped, leading to contentious and sometimes hilarious situations, as when a terrorist escaped from India to a neighbouring country, or one that was based abroad entered India. In such cases, both claimed jurisdiction over the man, sometimes insisting that he be 'handed over' with all intelligence gathered till that time. This turf war had been going on since the birth of RAW, and will probably never end, since both have separate reporting channels. The IB comes under the Home Ministry, while the RAW is part of the Cabinet Secretariat, and reports to the Prime Minister. The reluctance of the two agencies to share intelligence is perhaps the greatest weakness of the system, and has often acted to the detriment of the country's interests.

One of the first things that I noticed when I joined RAW was the obsession with security, most of which was misplaced. Of course, none of the doors had nameplates, or even the designations of the occupants. If one went to meet someone on some official work, and he happened to be out of his office, it was impossible to meet someone else, unless one returned to his own office, went through the directory, and found the room number of the concerned officer. I had an office on the 4th floor, with my PA being located about five rooms away. Of the four directors working under me, one was on the 3rd, one on the 4th and two on the 8th floor. It was only after about six months that I discovered the identities of persons sitting in rooms next door and across the corridor. Of course, one did get used to it after some time, but during the first few months, it caused a lot of irritation. Since no outsider entered the building, the reason for not putting the designation of the officer or his staff outside did not appear very convincing. The practice in Defence Headquarters is to write the designation outside the door, without the name. On the other hand, in the Ministry of External Affairs one finds only the name, without the designation. RAW had neither. An interesting feature was the presence of a doormat and two flower pots outside the rooms of officers of the rank of joint secretary and above. Apparently, this was to prevent junior staff from accidentally barging in and disturbing senior officers!

Another noticeable feature was the reluctance to use the words RAW in conversation or correspondence. Even when it had to be mentioned, it was always R&AW, and not RAW. For some reason, omitting the 'and' was frowned upon. I could not find any logic for this, since the 'and' was usually omitted in most other abbreviations, such as DRDO, IDSA, etc. Perhaps it was the negative connotation of the word 'raw' that was behind this practice. In conversation and correspondence, the organization was always referred to as Cabinet Secretariat, and never by its own designation. This was true even in meetings held with other security and intelligence agencies or government departments. Surprisingly, the IB did not seem to have any such hang up, and neither did others such as Military Intelligence, Signals Intelligence and SPG, etc. As was to be expected, the department had a number of stations in foreign countries. These were usually referred to by three letter code signs, such as ABC, XYZ, RST, etc. The code signs were designed for use in messages or telegrams that were sent outside, as a security measure. They were certainly not meant for use within the office, in conversation or correspondence. However, I found that everyone used them even in internal notings and discussions. Apart from causing confusion, little else was achieved. I recall that I had to frequently ask the person who used the code sign to identify the station he was referring to. In fact, this actually amounted to a breach of security, since the name of the place and the codeword both were used in the same conversation or telephone line.

The working hours were from 9.30 a.m. to 6.00 p.m., with a lunch break from 1 to 2 p.m. For the first few days, I reached the office dot on time. However, I found the office still being cleaned, and most of the staff yet to arrive. Another difficulty was that there were long queues outside the lifts, and most of those who worked on the lower floors preferred to walk up the three or four flights of stairs. When I mentioned this to a colleague, he smiled, and told me that senior officers were not expected to come before 10 a.m. I found that his advice was sensible. By 10 a.m. the crowd outside the lifts had dwindled, the rooms were cleaned and most of the staff had arrived. Of course, the departure timings were also staggered accordingly. Most of the subordinate staff used chartered buses to commute, and began thinning out at about 5.30 p.m. Officers who came in their cars normally left at around 6 p.m., while those entitled to staff cars left a little later. A few had to stay on until late at night, especially if there was something important to do. The lights on the tenth and eleventh floors, which housed the top rung of the hierarchy, were rarely switched off before 9 or 10 p.m.

Within the first few months, I had begun to form an opinion, which grew stronger with the years, that the organization was bloated, top heavy and expensive. Since the only other organization I was familiar with was the Army, I automatically used it as a yardstick to make comparisons. Due to the difference in role and tasking, this sometimes led to wrong conclusions, which had to be modified. However, when I made the comparison between Army Signals and the Telecom Division, the results were more realistic. The first thing that struck me was the large number of senior officers at the headquarters. There were more than 25 officers of the rank of joint secretary and above, in Delhi alone. In the Directorates of Military and Signals Intelligence, which have similar roles, the number of officers above the rank of major general is just four.

In the Telecom Division, there were four officers above the rank of joint secretary, including three on deputation. The total manpower of the Telecom Division was about 1600. In an Army Command, which has about 20,000 Signals personnel, there is only one Signals major general. Out of the four directors under me, one (he was a brigadier) was looking after communications, which included the signal centre and radio transmitters and receivers. In a corps or divisional signal regiment, a major would have done the some job. Army HQ Signals, in Delhi, has communications facilities that are ten or twenty times larger than what we had in RAW, yet a brigadier was looking after them.

The reasons for the large size of the department were many. One was that it functioned like a typical government department, with fixed hours of work, holidays, leave entitlements, overtime and so on. I was surprised to find that vehicles of some senior officers were assigned two or three drivers, since each worked only for 8 hours. The same applied to personal staff, which had to be duplicated or triplicated. The CRF (Central Repair Facility) held about 200 drivers, 50 mechanics and 200 miscellaneous personnel, to drive and maintain less than 100 vehicles. Even then, most of the repairs had to be done outside, in the market. Subordinate staff did not work on Saturdays or Sundays. If they were called to work on weekends or holidays, they had to be given a day off in lieu, or compensated monetarily. Anyone kept in the office after 6 p.m. was entitled to overtime allowance. Of course, curtailing leave was unthinkable. It was availed of as a matter of right, and not a privilege. Nobody's service was ever terminated for absence without leave (In the Army, after 30 days absence the man is declared a deserter and discharged from service).

There appeared to be considerable difference in the workload of officers and subordinate staff. While the doors of officers were normally shut, in larger rooms housing other workers the doors were usually left open. While walking through corridors, it was a common sight to see people reading newspapers or chatting. Coffee and tea vends were available in the lobby after every three floors, and these were always crowded. After a giant TV screen was installed in the main lobby on the ground floor, it was surrounded by a crowd of viewers at all times, especially if a cricket match was going on. Soon after I joined, a canteen was opened in the CRF, where personnel could buy stores and groceries at Army canteen rates. This proved to be a very popular venture, and was always crowded. How the canteen came about makes an interesting story, which is recounted later in this chapter.

Another feature of RAW was the large number of cadres that existed, especially among the junior staff. The bulk of the manpower was from the GD (general duties) cadre, who were known as 'junior executives.' The other cadres were telecom, secretarial, ministerial and accounts, crypto, cipher, technical research, language, economic research, information, political, cartographic, MT (mechanical transport), workshop and the CRF (Central Repair Facility). Some of these cadres were very small, numbering just 15 to 20 odd personnel, and one often wondered why they were created. The reason for having separate cadres for crypto and cipher was not clear, as was the case with CRF, MT and Workshop. Promotions in each cadre were based on vacancies, and this often led to heartburn and representations, when one overtook the other.

As was to be expected, a large number of personnel were stationed abroad. However, the locations of these stations did not appear to be based on intelligence considerations. The number of stations and personnel in Europe and the USA was larger than in the underdeveloped countries, with the African and South American continents being virtually ignored. A posting to one of the attractive stations was much sought after, arranging which consumed a substantial portion of the time and energy of most of the staff. The subordinate staff was able to get about one to two foreign assignments during their service, and tried very hard to get more. All of them had only one reason - money. Foreign allowances were considerably higher than what they were paid in India, and some even mentioned this in their applications, citing a daughter's marriage or building a house as valid reasons for being posted abroad. I found that most of the senior officers had done three to four stints abroad. In fact, the topic of conversation in most parties was usually about which station was due to fall vacant, who were the likely contenders, who stood a better chance and so on. Since the Secretary had a *carte blanche* in deciding these postings, proximity to the seat of power played an important role. This naturally bred a culture of sycophancy that has few parallels in any other government agency.

The Secretary wields enormous clout, not only in deciding postings but also tours. He can send anybody anywhere in the world at the drop of a hat, and most senior officers had at least half a dozen foreign jaunts every year, with the number increasing during the summer months. This facility was the source of envy of every other department of the Government of India, where even ministers and senior bureaucrats have to obtain clearance from the PMO and the Ministries of Finance and External affairs before proceeding on tours to foreign countries. Not surprisingly, anyone who had children studying in the USA or UK – the percentage is quite large - was able to visit them at government expense. During my three and a half years, I went abroad twice. On returning from my first trip, I put in a claim for hotel expenses, etc. I also claimed the amount spent on telephone calls, which I had made back to my office, or to the residences of my colleagues or subordinates, outside office hours. The claim was disallowed on some technical ground. When I protested, the Joint Secretary (SA) told me very cheerfully, "Don't worry, we will send you on a another trip abroad as soon as possible, and you can recover your losses." Another senior officer, who was due to retire, was asked if there was any particular place he wanted to visit. His daughter was studying in the US, so he was given a two-week holiday, all expenses paid. Incidentally, joint secretaries travel business class, while the Secretary travels first class. If one wants, he can take a companion free, since most airlines have a free companion scheme in business class. Naturally, they stay in the best hotels. (I stayed in the Mariott

Marquis in Times Square in New York and the Pan Pacific in Yokohama).

Of course, the funds allotted to RAW are not subject to audit. The Ministry of Finance knows how much money is spent by the organisation, but no one really knows how it is spent. The expenditure incurred on administration including salaries, allowances, buildings, maintenance, purchase of stores, transport etc., is naturally controlled and audited. But funds for acquisition of intelligence are kept out of the purview of such controls, for obvious reasons. A large amount of this is paid to sources (agents, spies, informers and moles) whose identity is known only to the officer who is running them. This system is followed by intelligence agencies all over the world. However, whether the amount is actually spent on actual intelligence work depends on the integrity of the concerned officers. One often heard murmurs and whispers that implied that there were black sheep in the flock. One story that I heard concerned an officer in a foreign mission who was paying for his daughter's education in a college abroad, classifying her as a 'source'. In normal circumstances, this sort of thing can only continue for two to three years, since the 'source' would have to be handed over to the new incumbent when the officer is transferred. But sources sometimes dry up and even vanish, without a trace.

Before I joined, I had imagined RAW to be full of hard-nosed, tough-as-nails agents, who took enormous risks and were undeterred by adversity and danger. However, most of the personnel I came across appeared to be soft, with a very low risk taking profile. The junior staff had got used to being mollycoddled and seemed reluctant to face danger and hardships. Of course, it was only a question of leadership, which most senior officers appeared to lack. Barely two months after I joined, a severe earthquake devastated several towns in Gujarat, including Bhuj, where a station was located. Though none of our personnel lost his life, the building and some of their equipment was damaged. The Joint Secretary (TM), RL

Verma, was immediately sent to Bhuj. He found the personnel traumatized and decided to close the station and evacuate all the staff to Delhi. When I heard about this I was surprised, since apparently nobody had been hurt. Since only the building had been damaged, I suggested that we shift the station to an alternate location. Having served in the area earlier, I knew that the Army had a brigade in Bhuj, and I offered to arrange for our detachment to be attached to the signal company, until our own accommodation was repaired. I had come to know that the brigade had also suffered extensive damage and many of their personnel, including families, were staying in tents. But I was sure that they would give us at least one room, if not two. However, my suggestion was not accepted, as Verma and other officers of TM Wing felt that none of the personnel were in a fit state to go back. The Adviser (Tele), Dr. VK Singh, could not bring himself to overrule the objections of Verma and his team, and went along with their recommendation. In the event, the station at Bhuj remained closed for over a year, until the accommodation was repaired. Such a thing would have never happened in the Army, or for that matter, in any other organisation with a modicum of self-respect and pride in its job.

Lack of leadership at the top was also responsible for the major fiasco that occurred when Rabinder Singh, a joint secretary in RAW, who was suspected to be a mole, escaped in 2004. Details of the episode are given in a subsequent chapter. However, the role of one of the key players in the drama, who was partly responsible for Rabinder's escape, and the lack of leadership at the top that played a part, is described here. In early 2001, Amar Bhushan returned from Tokyo and took over as Additional Secretary (Personnel), replacing Shanmugam who went on deputation to the Government of Mauritius. After the retirement of AS Dulat, Vikram Sood took over as Secretary, and CD Sahay and JK Sinha were promoted special secretaries. Amar Bhushan filed a complaint in the Central Administrative Tribunal (CAT), on the ground that in the IPS, he had been senior to both Sahay and Sinha. He was subsequently promoted special secretary, and posted as Special Secretary (SR) in Bikaner House, relieving Hari Shanker, who became Secretary (Security). However, Amar Bhushan did not give up his office in RAW. He simply changed his designation from Additional Secretary (Personnel) to Special Secretary (Personnel). He spent half his time in RAW and half in Bikaner House. Of course, this was done without the approval of the Department of Personnel and Training (DOPT), which orders all transfers and postings of senior bureaucrats in Delhi. I am not sure if he took the approval of the Secretary (R), but it is most unlikely. Anyway, since he attended all meetings and signed correspondence as Special Secretary (Personnel), it could not have been without the tacit concurrence of Vikram Sood, the Secretary at that time.

After some time, when Bedi left ARC to raise the National Technical Facilities Organisation (NTFO), Amar Bhushan was posted as his relief. However, he did not vacate his offices in Bikaner House and RAW. He was now wearing three hats - Special Secretary (Personnel) in RAW; Special Secretary (SR) in Bikaner House, and Special Secretary, ARC. He began shuttling between the three offices, refusing to give up any of them. It was only when Ajay Singh was reverted from the Ministry of External Affairs and posted as Additional Secretary (SR) that Amar Bhushan left Bikaner House. By this time CD Sahay had taken over as Secretary (R). Though there was little love lost between the two, Sahay did not have the gumption to tell Amar Bhushan to stay out of RAW. This played an important part in facilitating the escape of Rabinder Singh, as will be described in a subsequent chapter. It was only when Sahay was on the verge of being sacked himself that he could build up the nerve to show Amar Bhushan the door.

A few months after I joined, Major Ram Dass came to my office. He was an ex-EME officer who was looking after the CRF (Central Repair Facility), which was responsible for providing vehicles to everyone in the organisation. He wanted me to counter sign an application from RAW for opening a CSD (Canteen Stores Department) canteen. As is well known, the CSD caters for personnel of the armed forces, who are exempted from paying sales tax on goods purchased by them through the CSD. The application from RAW was based on the premise that it had a large number of ex-servicemen, who found it inconvenient to go to the Station Canteen, which was quite far away. I asked Ram Dass why he was not getting it signed by Major General PK Puri, the Chief Military Intelligence Adviser, who was the senior Army officer present. Dass told me that according to the rules, only a serving major general could countersign the application. Since General Puri had retired, and was re-employed, he could not sign it. I countersigned the application, without further ado.

After a few months, the canteen was inaugurated, with much fanfare. It was the brainchild of Amar Bhushan, who had recently taken over as Additional Secretary (Personnel). Circulars were issued and notices regarding opening of the canteen were put up. However, I found that instead of catering exclusively to ex-servicemen, the canteen was open to all employees. In fact, very few ex-servicemen used the facility, preferring to go to the canteen to which they were attached for drawing their liquor quota. At the next annual conference, Amar Bhushan, who had now assumed the appointment of Special Secretary (Personnel), grandly announced the opening of the canteen, among the various welfare measures that he had introduced after had taken over. He was applauded warmly for this achievement, which had been tried unsuccessfully several times earlier.

After a few months, Ram Dass came to me again, this time with an application that the RAW canteen should be permitted to stock liquor and also high value items such refrigerators, air conditioners, motorcycles, cars, etc. According to the prevalent rules, ex-servicemen were attached either to the station canteen or another major canteen close to their place of residence for purchase of liquor. The quota was fixed, and the canteen was released only enough liquor to meet the authorised quota of ex-servicemen who were attached to it. As regards high value items, the procedure was that the person who wished to purchase a particular item placed a firm demand, along with a bank draft payable to the CSD, which then issued a release order on the dealer. The item was collected directly from the dealer, who was reimbursed by the CSD. Since sales tax on such items was either exempted or substantially reduced, the cost paid by the ex-serviceman was much lower than the market rate. Having seen the manner in which the canteen was functioning, I was certain that the facility would be misused. I refused to countersign the application, and Ram Dass went away crestfallen. I am not sure who finally countersigned the application, but apparently the request was not granted.

In June 2004, shortly before I retired, a circular was issued giving out the salient features of the Canteen Rules. There was to be Governing Council, chaired by Amar Bhushan, whose designation was shown as Special Secretary (Pers), RAW and Special Secretary (ARC). There was also an Executive Council, which was headed by the Vice Chairman, Niraj Srivastava, the Joint Secretary (Pers), who reported to Amar Bhushan. The third tier comprised the Advisory Committee, which had two representatives each from Groups A, B, C and D. Surprisingly, there was not a single ex-serviceman in any of the three committees. In fact, the word 'ex-serviceman' did not occur even once in the seven-page circular.

This was not all. The circular clearly stated that the privilege of purchasing goods from the canteen was available to all serving and retired employees of RAW and ARC, and others who may be authorised by the Executive Committee. According to the rules applicable to all canteens, they are subject to a quarterly audit by a board of officers from outside, ordered by the Station Headquarters. There was no such audit being carried out in RAW. Similarly, the canteen profit is to be utilized for welfare of officers and men, in the ratio of their purchases from the canteen. According to the circular, 10% and 65 % respectively would be transferred to the welfare funds of ARC and RAW, with the remaining 25% being retained by the canteen for development and expansion.

It now became clear that RAW had resorted to a subterfuge by using the ex-servicemen to get a canteen sanctioned for their own personnel who were not entitled to such facilities. Since I had been partly responsible for this, I felt I must inform the concerned authorities. Accordingly, I wrote a DO letter to the Quarter Master General, Army Headquarters, informing him of the anomalies in the canteen being run by RAW. I feared that after some time, other security agencies and para military forces would make similar demands, leading to further misuse of the facility. In the long run, the facility might be withdrawn from everyone, including the armed forces. If RAW was to run a canteen, it should cater only for entitled personnel, i.e. ex-servicemen. I wrote a similar DO letter to the GOC Delhi Area, who was directly responsible for all canteens in his area, including prevention of misuse and audit. I am not sure what action was taken in the matter. With its penchant for getting around rules, I am sure RAW would have found a way to continue the canteen.

Another achievement that Amar Bhushan was proud of was designing the RAW emblem. All security and law enforcing agencies have a crest or badge that is worn on the cap as part of the uniform. The emblem is used in the official letter-head of the organisation and is also displayed on vehicles, blazers, neck ties, scarves etc. RAW did not have an emblem, and Amar Bhushan decided that it must have one. A specialist designer was commissioned with the project of creating a suitable logo. The new emblem was inaugurated at a grand function held in the auditorium, where an assortment of objects bearing the new crest was displayed. Of course, this was the last time we were to see the emblem. Due to security reasons, it could not be used on letter-heads and neither could we use it on vehicles or on attire. Some diehards bought a few crested whiskly glasses and dinner plates, but these also could be used only in the presence of colleagues. At the end, it turned out to be a futile exercise, after spending lakhs of rupees, most of it towards the cost of design.

4

The Telecom Division

The Telecom Division in RAW performs functions similar to those of Signals in the Army. These functions fall in two broad divisions – communications and interception. I noticed that unlike the armed forces, RAW did not have its own communication networks, except for an internal radio network for clearance of message traffic to stations within the country, and external radio links with a few foreign stations. For telephone communications, it was totally dependant on the Department of Telecommunications (DOT). Data communications were virtually non-existent. Teleprinters were used for passing messages to the larger stations, on circuits hired from the DOT. These stations were in turn connected to smaller stations by similar links. For the majority of small stations, the only means of communications was radio, which enabled only passage of messages after encryption. Voice communication with outstations was possible only on telephone, using STD. A few senior functionaries in headquarters and foreign missions had desktop encryption devices, which provided medium grade security. However, this equipment was purchased from abroad, and their reliability was doubtful.

Like other intelligence agencies, RAW relied heavily on interception of communications. In fact, officers in the Telecom Division often boasted that 90% of the intelligence gathered by RAW was from technical means, with the human element providing the balance 10%. If this was indeed true, the resources provided to the Telecom Division, in the form of manpower and equipment, were certainly not in conformity with the results achieved, when compared with the other organs. There were just two officers who had a B Tech or BE degree. Most of the officers had risen through the ranks, and had obtained engineering qualifications through the Institute of Engineers or the Institute of Telecom Engineers. Most of them were Science graduates in Electronics. Fortunately, there was a large number of ex-servicemen among the junior staff, at the level of Field Officer (Tele) and Deputy Field Officer (Tele). The retirement age in the Army being comparatively lower, they completed their colour service and retired from the Army when they were about 45 years old. Joining RAW gave them an opportunity to serve for another 15 years, which was an attractive proposition. What is more, they continued to get their full Army pension, along with their salary from RAW. Strangely enough, this benefit was not available to officers, whose pension was deducted while fixing their salaries on re-employment with RAW. Most of these ex servicemen had served in Army Signals for 15-20 years, and were fully conversant with the equipment being used in RAW for communications as well as interception. In fact, they formed the backbone of the Telecom Division of RAW during its initial years, and their gradual departure had begun to tell on the efficiency of the organisation.

The Telecom Division was headed by the Additional Secretary (Tele), Dr. VK Singh, who was also known as the Adviser (Tele). I learned that he was on deputation from Doordarshan, and thus somewhat of an 'outsider'. After he left, there was no permanent incumbent for quite some time. As a result, every thing had to go up CD Sahay, the Special

Secretary (W). He was an extremely busy man and could rarely devote more than a few minutes each day to matters concerning the Telecom Division. Fortunately, he had some knowledge of electronics, having studied the subject as a science graduate. After a few months one of the additional secretaries, Rishpal Singh, was asked to look after the job in addition to his normal duties. Being a generalist, his knowledge of technical matters was naturally limited, and this inhibited his interest and involvement in the Telecom Division. It was only when PV Kumar took over that the Telecom Division had a full time head. Like Rishpal, Kumar was also from the operational cadre. He had graduated as a civil engineer and was also unable to fully comprehend the technical details of systems and equipment being used and considered for procurement. The three or four officers who were on deputation from Army Signals sometimes wondered at this ad hoc manner of functioning. It would be unthinkable to have an infantry or cavalry officer holding the appointment of head of Signals in the Army, or for a fighter pilot to look after a similar job in the Air Force.

Before I joined, RL Verma was the only joint secretary in the Telecom Division. In fact, before the arrival of Dr. VK Singh a few years earlier, Verma had been heading the Telecom Division, as the Joint Secretary (Tele). He was not exactly happy when the appointment was upgraded and he was relegated to the number two spot. However, he was still involved in all activities, and everything had to go through him. It was only when two more joint secretaries – VS Yadav and I – joined the Telecom Division in the year 2000 that he found his authority severely eroded. Logically, he should still have been looking after at least one third of all activities. However, Dr. VK Singh obtained the Secretary's approval for a fresh allocation of work to the three joint secretaries soon after we joined. According to this, Verma was designated Joint Secretary (Tele – TM); Yadav became Joint Secretary (Tele – SM) and I became Joint Secretary (Tele – TE/DM). The abbreviations TM, SM and DM stood for terrestrial monitoring, satellite monitoring, and data monitoring, while TE stood for telecom equipment, which essentially involved procurement. In addition to these broad divisions, several other important assignments, such as communications, cadre control, budgeting etc., were assigned to me. Each of us was also given four or five projects, under Vision 2000. As a result, I had four directors working under me, while Yadav and Verma had two each. Verma naturally protested violently at the loss of control over the important areas such as cadre control and budgeting, and these were subsequently given back to him.

In fact, both Yadav and I had come on deputation under Project Vision 2000, which had about 15 projects. In addition, four directors had also come on deputation, along with several deputy secretaries and under secretaries. Out of the 15 projects, only about seven or eight were then on the anvil, and it would have been logical to assign the deputationist officers to these projects, leaving the permanent cadre officers with their normal duties. Instead, most of the new projects were assigned to the permanent cadre officers, their duties being taken over by those who had come on deputation. There seemed to be no rationale for this at that time. It was only later that the reasons became clear. The new projects involved procurement of new equipment, with the opportunity of foreign trips. Procurements also involved large amounts of funds. Most of the senior officers had 'favourite' vendors, from whom equipment was purchased for the Telecom Division. The permanent cadre officers had to serve in the organization till they retired, and were more amenable to suggestions and recommendations from their superiors. On the other hand, the newcomers had come on deputation for a few years. They did not know any of the favorite vendors and neither could they be subjected to any pressure on this account.

The four directors on deputation under Vision 2000 were Brigadiers SC Anand and Yugesh Bhardwaj from the Army; SA

Kumar from the Ministry of Information Technology and VK Mittal from the DRDO. The directors from the Telecom cadre were K Rajagopalan, RR Manan, Sampath Krishna, SK Bali and Venugopalan, the last two being out of Delhi. In addition, Brigadiers SK Datta and Ujjal Dasgupta had been re-employed in RAW against regular vacancies. Datta was the Director (TE) while Dasgupta was Director (Computers). The latter appointment had recently been taken out of the Telecom Division, and placed directly under the Additional Secretary (Personnel).

Soon after he joined, Bhardwaj was appointed Director (Satcom), and made responsible for satellite communications. After floating around for a few months without any work being assigned to him, Anand was sent as officer in charge of the transmitter station at Patparganj, on the outskirts of Delhi. The previous incumbent had been only a deputy secretary! SA Kumar was designated Director (DM) and made in charge of Internet monitoring, which was still to be commissioned. Mittal was given a couple of projects that were still in the conceptual stage. Mannan continued as Director (TM) under Verma, while Rajagopalan became the Director (SM) under Yadav. Sampath had no specific job, and was told to look after the station in Patiala, under Yadav.

According to the distribution of work, I was responsible for procurement, data monitoring, and communications, both internal and external. In addition, I had to look after the relevant projects assigned to me under the Vision 2000, for which I had been deputed, but about which I knew nothing. I asked Datta if someone was going to brief me about my job, and was surprised when he replied in the negative. I then took it up with the Adviser (Telecom), who replied in the same vein, asking me to find out whatever I wanted to know from the concerned Director. As regards details of Vision 2000, he told me that it was Top Secret, and I could go through the relevant extracts, which were in a file held in the custody of Brigadier Datta.

Needless to say, I was shocked. I had expected that each of my subordinates would give me a detailed briefing about his specific field, along with the ongoing projects and the problems he was facing. Instead, I was expected to call each one to my office and ask searching questions. There was no formal visit to the facilities that I was expected to oversee. I was expected to visit them at my convenience. Since I did not even know what these facilities were, or what they did or where they were located, this was indeed a strange way to learn about them. I expressed my misgivings to Brigadier Datta, who could do little more than smile, telling me that I would soon get used to the way the organisation functioned. Of course, he himself gave me a detailed briefing about the procurement section, which he was looking after. In fact, this was the only proper briefing I received.

Apart from the apparent lack of coordination in the professional area, I found that the administration was equally disjointed. I did not have an office for almost a month, and sat in Brigadier Datta's office during this period. I got a residential telephone more than a month after I occupied the house, and that too only after I spoke to someone in Army HQ Signals, who got it done within two days. I did not get my full complement of personal staff such as Personal Secretary (PS), Personal Assistant (PA) and FAs (field assistants) for several months. I did not get a staff car, which joint secretaries are entitled to, and it was only after several visits to the office of the Additional Secretary (Pers) that he agreed to hire a few taxis, until the cars could be made available. However, these were withdrawn after the arrival of the new Additional Secretary (Pers), Mr. Amar Bhushan, who felt that it was a security risk. He substituted the taxis with pick-and-drop, with three officers sharing one staff car. Similar glitches were faced with regard to office equipment such as computers, printers and photocopiers. Of course, there was no air conditioner in my office, which had earlier been used by someone who was not entitled to one. This was a far cry from the way things were done in the Army. After a couple of months, I got a distinct impression that the difficulties I was facing were primarily because I was an 'outsider', and I began to have second thoughts about my decision to join the RAW.

When things did not improve for several months, I put up a note to the Secretary in April 2001, bringing to his notice the state of affairs. I pointed out that during the 36 years I had spent in the Army, I had lived in tents and bunkers, and could withstand considerable hardship and discomfort, provided it was unavoidable and shared by everyone. However, I was not ready to accept shabby treatment and humiliation of the sort I had been subjected to for the last few months. Since RAW was not in a position to provide me the staff and perquisites that I was entitled to, I requested that my deputation may be terminated and I should be reverted to my parent department. After a few days, I received a call from the Secretary's office, informing me that he wanted to se me. Vikram Sood was apologetic, and asked me to reconsider my decision. He assured me that if things did not improve within a week, I was at liberty to go back. He was as good as his word - things did improve, and I got the personal staff, office equipment, staff car and air conditioner. In fact, Amar Bhushan told the concerned under secretary to install one in my office within 24 hours, and if he could not lay his hands on one, he could take out one from his office, since he had two.

Bit by bit, I began to come to grips with the job. After visiting the signal centre, transmitter station, the local monitoring stations and the technical stores, I was quite depressed. They were all in a fairly run down state as regards the surrounding area, buildings, furniture, fitments, etc. I spoke to Dr. VK Singh and told him that I would like to take a few selected officers on a tour of similar facilities of the Army in Delhi. After obtaining his concurrence, I spoke to my colleagues in the Signals Directorate in Army HQ, who agreed to the proposal. I took team of about a dozen officers to the communication centre in Sena Bhawan, followed by a visit to the VSAT terminal and telephone exchange in Signals Enclave on Rao Tula Ram Marg. This was the first time many of the officers had seen the Army Signals facilities, and they came away suitably impressed and educated. I told them that if they were able to bring up our own facilities to even half the standards we had seen, it would be an achievement.

For some strange reason, the telephone exchange was not part of the signal centre. The exchange functioned under Director (TM) while the signal centre was under Director (TC), both being under different joint secretaries. An even greater anomaly was ciphers, which was not part of the Telecom Division. In RAW, there were separate cadres for crypto and cipher staff, both under the Joint Secretary (Crypto), who did not report to the Adviser (Tele). The crypto personnel were mainly employed for crypto analysis, i.e. code breaking. Cipher staff was used for encoding and decoding our own messages. Logically, the cipher office or crypto centre should have been part of the signal centre, for ease of handling and saving of time. In RAW, this was not the case, and messages were physically carried from the signal centre to the cipher wing, which was on a different floor. This naturally resulted in delays, which could have been avoided if they had been co-located. I tried to remedy the situation but ran into a brick wall in the person of Prasada Rao, the Joint Secretary (Crypto), who zealously guarded his turf and refused to budge.

During my visit to the signal centre I was informed that almost every message was being graded secret and being given the highest priority. This put an unnecessary load on the cipher staff and also increased the time for transmission. When I asked for the standing orders I was told that there were none. Any officer could initiate a top secret or secret message and give whatever priority he wished to. I was indeed upset when I heard this. There was no way of ensuring that important messages were cleared first. I was also surprised to find that no one seemed to be perturbed if a message was delayed, even for two or three days. The Under Secretary in charge of the signal centre rarely bothered to inform anyone if a circuit was down, especially on a holiday. Perhaps he had realized that no senior officer liked to be disturbed by such mundane occurrences, especially when he could not do much about it. This was in stark contrast to what prevailed in the Army. I remembered my days as a young officer, when I had to give hourly reports to my company commander or commanding officer in case messages were being delayed or circuits were down, at all hours of the day and night.

I discovered that most of my time was spent in matters dealing with procurement. According to the existing procedure, the concerned branch or wing of the Telecom Division – TM, SM or DM – submitted a demand for equipment that it considered necessary to carry out its functions. The type of equipment, including technical parameters and quantity, were included in the demand, along with the approximate cost and list of likely suppliers. The demand was vetted by the Technical Advisory Group (TAG), which ensured that the technical specifications were realistic and in conformity with the purpose for which it was being procured. It was then submitted to the Secretary, through the Adviser (Tele), for obtaining 'administrative approval'. Once this had been obtained, the demand was sent to the procurement cell, which sent it to Finance, for their concurrence. After confirming that the amount was within the allocated budget, and that the prices quoted were reasonable, Finance returned it to the procurement cell, which prepared the draft Request For Proposal (RFP), in consultation with the user, and sent it to the Purchase Cell in Bikaner House, for further processing.

The Purchase Cell was headed by the Assistant Director (Purchase Cell), who functioned under the Director (R), who was part of the set up headed by the Special Secretary (R), in Bikaner House. The purchase cell sent out the Request for Proposal (RFP) or tender enquiry to selected vendors, and once these were received, constituted the Technical Evaluation Committee (TEC) and the Price Negotiation Committee (PNC).

The vendors submitted the bids in two parts, with the first part containing the technical parameters of the equipment and the second part having the financial bid. Once the TEC had gone through the technical bids, which often involved technical presentations and demonstrations, it short-listed the vendors whose equipment met the specifications. The financial bids of these short-listed firms were then·opened, and the one having the lowest bid was selected. The file was then put up again to the Secretary, through Finance for his approval. The 'expenditure sanction' indicated the exact cost of the equipment, the vendor from whom it was to be bought, the delivery schedule and various other clauses dealing with warranties, after sales service, training, etc. After obtaining the expenditure sanction the Purchase Cell issued the Acceptance of Tender (AT), which constituted the order to the vendor to deliver the equipment. In most cases, the cost was paid though an irrevocable letter of credit, which became effective once the item had been shipped or dispatched. Once the equipment was ready, the user sent a team to the manufacturers' premises to carry out the Factory Acceptance Test (FAT), to confirm that the equipment was functioning properly. In case of new equipment, some officers were also trained on the equipment, by the manufacturer. Once the acceptance tests were over, the vendor was asked to ship the items. The letter of credit was released as soon as the equipment was free on board (FOB), indicating that it had been loaded on a ship or aircraft.

The procedure being followed was in conformity with guidelines issued by the Central Vigilance Commission (CVC). However, there were several anomalies. According the rules, which were unwritten, no one in RAW was permitted to correspond with outside agencies, including vendors. All interaction, through telephone or letters was conducted by the set up in Bikaner House. This resulted in delays, apart from unnecessary paper work. The other difficulty was in obtaining budgetary quotes, which were necessary to arrive at the approximate price of the equipment. This was the responsibility of the indenting wing of the Telecom Division. However, in view of the embargo on correspondence with outside agencies, this was extremely difficult. As a result, usually the price at which similar equipment had been procured earlier formed the basis for the budgetary estimate. Since the prices of electronic equipment usually decreased, with time, this often led to inflated estimates. Also, the method could not be used for new equipment, which was the type that was required most of the time. The RFPs were sent only to a selected list of vendors, with the result that new companies were seldom included.

I made an attempt to solve or at least alleviate some of these difficulties. When I asked if there was any written order regarding the ban on correspondence with outside agencies, no one was able to produce it, but everyone was vehement that it was not permitted. I learned that sometimes officers used their personal e-mails to get the required quotes, which I thought was highly irregular. After this, I began corresponding directly with companies, whenever required. I also used my official e-mail address, and told the officers in the Procurement Cell to follow suit. I suggested to the Adviser (Tele) and Bikaner House that we resort to the open tender system, and publish the tender enquiries in the newspapers, as was being done by other intelligence and security agencies such as the IB and the SPG. However, this was not agreed to, on the grounds of security. Since the RFPs under the existing system were being sent to several foreign companies, this argument was not really valid. Foreign intelligence agencies would certainly come to know the type of equipment that we were buying, through the companies based in the respective countries. Then what was the harm in Indian companies knowing about it? It appeared that the objections stemmed from vested interests, rather than considerations of security.

I found that the time taken for the entire process of procurement was unduly long. It most cases, three to four years elapsed before the equipment was finally delivered. In some cases, it took even longer. With the pace of advancement in technology, especially in electronics, such delays were unacceptable, since the equipment was already obsolete or obsolescent when it was brought into use. This point was deliberated at length and the Special Secretary (W), Mr. CD Sahay, ordered that a committee be formed to suggest ways and means to reduce the time taken in the procurement process. Brigadier Yugesh Bhardwaj, who chaired the committee, put in a lot of effort and came up with a suggested solution, but it could not be implemented, due to objections raised by many of the agencies involved, including Finance and the Purchase Cell in Bikaner House.

Once a month, the Adviser (Tele) held a conference in his office to monitor the progress on procurement of equipment. The conference was attended by the Joint Secretary (TE/DM), i.e me; the Director (TE), Brigadier SK Datta; and the deputy or under secretaries in he Procurement Cell, dealing with various types of equipment. The conference usually took several hours, because of the large number of items, some of which were pending for almost five years. In most cases the delays were on the part of the Purchase Cell, and I suggested that the concerned officers should also attend the conference. This became possible only after Rishpal Singh took over as Adviser (Tele). Being from the operational branch, he apparently had more clout than Dr. VK Singh, who was a technocrat. However, due to reasons already explained, the conferences were not held regularly. Matters really improved only after PV Kumar took over. The Director (R), SK Mehrotra, and the Assistant Director (Purchase Cell), Gaurav Sharma, began to attend the conferences regularly. In addition the joint secretary and the director of the indenting unit also began to attend. This ensured that the blame for delays was not passed to someone in absentia, as had been happening earlier.

I remember an interesting matter that came up during one of the first procurement conferences that I attended. There were two items that were unduly delayed. When asked the reason for the delay, Brigadier Datta mentioned that the file was with the Joint Secretary (TM), Mr. RL Verma. I saw from the record that the files had been with him for over a year. I was surprised, and queried Brigadier Datta as to why he had not asked him to return them. Brigadier Datta said that he had spoken to him several times, without success. I made a note and told the Adviser that I would talk to Mr. Verma as soon as the conference was over. After I returned to my office, I spoke to Verma on the telephone and asked him about the files. He said he would return them shortly. In the event, he did not, even after I spoke to him three or four times. Finally, I sent him a written note, without success.

When I asked Brigadier Datta if he knew why Verma was not returning the files, he only smiled. After talking to some others, I found that everyone in the Telecom Division knew the reason. Apparently Verma was keen that the equipment should be bought from Rohde and Schwarz, a German firm, while the Adviser had short-listed another firm, which was more to his liking. I was told that Rohde and Schwarz was Verma's favourite company, and as long as he is there, he will make sure that no one else gets the order. I was shocked when I heard this, but as subsequent events were to prove, this was true. Verma handed over the files only when he retired, more than a year later. By then, the quotations and sanctions had become outdated, and the case had to be shelved. More than the unwillingness of Verma to hand over the files, what surprised me was the reluctance of the Adviser to put him on the mat for it. It was nothing but blatant disobedience of orders, which should have invited instant retribution. As I was to discover, leadership was not one of the qualities that one could find easily in RAW.

The reluctance of senior officers to take action against erring subordinates appeared to be strange, considering that it was an intelligence agency, where responsibility had to be fixed in case of lapses. I recall a case where two computers that were part of a newly acquired system were found missing during transshipment from the Central Stores to the outstation. The Additional Secretary (Tele) asked Brigadier Anand to conduct an inquiry, which held certain individuals responsible for the loss. However, no action was taken against the individuals, other than a verbal reprimand. In another instance, during a visit to the transmitter station, I found certain equipment in wooden crates. On enquiring from the officer in charge, it was revealed that these contained brand new antennae, which had been purchased several years earlier, but had never been used. When I went back to headquarters I brought this to the notice of the Additional Secretary (Tele). It appeared to be a criminal waste of money, and I felt that the officer who had placed the demand should be asked to explain. It was discovered that the concerned officer had since retired, and since no use could be found for the antennae, these had to be condemned. Later, when I was presiding officer of a condemnation board, I found several items lying in the stores, still in their original packing cases. It appeared that there was no mechanism to check the actual need for smaller equipment and accessories, which were often purchased even when they were not required, causing loss to the government.

The unwillingness to take action naturally resulted in deterioration in discipline. Once, when I was to proceed to another city by an early morning flight, a car was detailed by Control to pick up SA Kumar, who was accompanying me, and then come to my house, to pick me up. When the car did not arrive in time, I rang up Kumar's residence. He told me that the vehicle had reached, but the driver got involved in a scuffle with the security guard, after he grazed a parked vehicle. They arrived after about 15 minutes, and I hurriedly got into the car. I found that the driver was drunk, and was driving dangerously. Since I preferred to miss the flight rather than reach a hospital, I told him to drive very slowly. We reached the airport in the nick of time, and could catch the flight only because we did not have any baggage. On my return, I complained to the CRF, but found that they were not willing to take any action, other than giving the driver a warning. I spoke to several other officers, who told me that the particular driver was a 'bad hat' and that is the reason no one wanted him as his staff car driver. One driver, who was an ex-serviceman, told me that most of the drivers in the Control pool spent their time drinking and gambling, even when on duty. When I asked him how they were able to afford it, he told me that most of them sold petrol in the market. I decided to put it in writing and sent a note to the Additional Secretary (Pers). It appeared that they were waiting for someone to complain against the driver, so that they could throw him out, which they did.

As soon as I had settled down, I began going on tours to visit the stations located outside Delhi. One of the first places I visited was Ladakh and Kashmir followed by the North East. Of course I had served in these areas during my Army service and was quite familiar with the terrain and living conditions. However, I must confess that I was shocked at the living conditions of some of the RAW detachments. Even in the most inhospitable regions, the Army tries to ensure that the troops get proper food, clothing and living quarters. RAW did not have any administrative infrastructure of its own, and had to depend on the Army, BSF or local civil government officials for its administrative requirements. Because of the nature of their job, our men could not mix freely with the locals or the units of security forces in the area. As a result, some of them were quite isolated and also uncomfortable. In most of the smaller detachments, the men had to do their own cooking and washing, apart from their professional tasks. The supply of rations was uncertain, and depended a lot on the initiative and local liaison established by the person in charge of the detachment. Worst of all, they did not have any secure means of communication with their bases, and had to use the civil telephone system or the communication network of the Army.

I tried to resolve some of the problems regarding accommodation, rations and transport with the local Army or BSF units, all of whom were very helpful. The conditions in other areas, such as Southern and Western India were much better, with almost all the personnel staying in proper built up accommodation with their families. However, I noticed that in most places, the stations were not sited properly. It appeared that administrative constraints had been kept in mind rather than technical considerations. In a particular VHF monitoring station in Ladakh I found that they were not getting anything worthwhile from across the border because they were located in a valley, next to a *gompa*. The men agreed that they would get better results if they went to the top of the hill or the pass that was located on the watershed. But this was not possible due to administrative problems. I spoke to the Army formation commander and he readily agreed to attach our personnel to the units located on the heights.

When I visited a station located in a port town, I found that it was housed in a very large three-storey building located next to the sea. The house was built on a steep slope in a heavily populated area, and surrounded by houses on all sides. As a result, radio transmissions were screened by the hillside and other buildings in the vicinity. The building was very large and only about one third of it was being used. It was most unsuitable for use as a monitoring station. When I asked the officer in charge the reason for selecting the particular building his answer stunned me. The building belonged to a gentleman who was a close relative of a senior officer in our organisation. It had been taken on lease at an abnormally high rent. The local officer in charge had protested but his objections were overruled and the building hired. The town had excellent locations where the station could have been sited, but the worst one was chosen.

During most of my visits I stayed in a 'safe house' that was usually a hired building. In almost all stations, these had been converted into guesthouses, where senior visiting officers from headquarters were accommodated. Before I left, I always asked for a mess bill, as was customary in the Army. Not once was I given a bill, even when I insisted. I still do not know who paid for hospitality, but I have a lurking suspicion that it was from secret funds. After a couple of such visits, I began to stay in an Army mess, if one was located nearby. When this was not possible, I preferred to stay with the BSF or in a PWD inspection bungalow or government guesthouse. It was only when none of these options was available that I agreed to become a 'source' for a short while.

Another custom in vogue was for the senior officer in the station to invite the visiting officer to his home for dinner or lunch. Often, it put the host's family to some inconvenience, but it was difficult to refuse such invitations. In some cases, the senior officer at the station insisted on hosting a dinner in an expensive restaurant, in addition to the customary meal in his home. I was told that this was the norm when senior officers went on foreign visits. Apparently, the expenditure was charged to funds available with the station head for this purpose. This also gave the officer and his family a chance to enjoy a meal in a fancy restaurant, which they probably would not be able to afford on their own.

During my visits to outstations I made it known that I preferred to have a meal with all the staff in the station premises itself, something like a 'barakhana' that is normally held in Army units. This not only gives an opportunity for the visiting officer to meet everyone informally, but is also an excellent method of getting feedback regarding the problems being faced by them. In some stations I found the officer in charge of the station reluctant to hold such informal gatherings. This was probably due to a fear that subordinate staff would air their grievances against him, or bring out irregularities. Whenever I found such undercurrents, I tried to get it out of the senior officer himself, before talking to the staff. Of course, any one who had a problem which could be resolved at headquarters was asked to give it in writing, which I conveyed to the concerned officer on my return to Delhi. Most of these problems related to pay, allowances, postings, promotions etc, which concerned the personnel and administrative department. I found that if taken up at the appropriate level, the majority of problems could be solved without much effort. In some cases the problems had to be resolved with local authorities or outside agencies. I took these up with the Commissioner or Additional Commissioner when I met him after visiting the stations in his jurisdiction.

One thing that struck me at almost all stations was the lack of attention to 'signalmanship', as it is called in the Army. Just as a good workman takes pride in his 'workmanship, and a good craftsman in his 'craftsmanship', signallers or communicators take pride in signalmanship, which essentially means maintaining high standards of professional work and keeping things shipshape. I often found antenna masts leaning or bent, the guy ropes loose, and the antenna wire sagging. When I asked the persons responsible the reason for this I sometimes got stunning answers. At one station in the North East where it rained heavily, the men were reluctant to go near the mast because they feared snakes in the undergrowth. When I asked the station in charge what he intended to do about it, he told me that he had put in a bid for labour, and as soon as he received the sanction he would get the grass removed. At another station the tin roof of the generator shed had been damaged, and they were waiting for the PWD to replace it.

While one could probably overlook uncut grass and damaged tin roofs, what could not be condoned was neglect of basic rules of signalmanship such loose cable joints, unsecured electric wires, broken earth wires, incorrect aerial lengths and so on. At one station I found them using a dipole aerial to communicate on radio with Delhi. The length of the aerial seemed to indicate that it was used for a day frequency. When I asked for the night frequency aerial, I was told that they did not have one. The reason given was lack of space - night frequencies are lower, needing longer aerials – but I was not convinced. I asked the station incharge if he had heard of a triple folded dipole antenna, which could be used over a wide band of frequencies. He had, but said that he did not have one, and neither had he placed a demand for it. It was just plain laziness on the part of the station incharge, who naturally got a well-deserved mouthful from me. It also came to light that the station had not been visited by any officer from Delhi for several years, which accounted for the lackadaisical attitude of the personnel there.

Though all stations were supposed to be inspected annually, it appeared that some had not been visited for several years. When I pointed this out, the TM Wing, under whose jurisdiction most of the stations functioned, came up with the answer that they did not have enough officers, which was true. I suggested to the Additional Secretary (Tele) that instead of sending only officers from TM Wing, we should make use of all officers in the Telecom Division. For my part, I volunteered to make all officers working under me available for this task, and inspect a few stations myself. This was accepted, and thereafter an annual inspection programme was drawn up, with each officer inspecting three or four stations. The system proved of great value, bringing to light several problems that had been pending for long. TM Wing initially had some reservations, since the inspecting officers often pointed out deficiencies and anomalies that they were partly responsible for. However, they later came round to appreciate the advantages of the system, which enabled them to keep a closer watch over their stations.

Another glaring lacunae that I noticed was in the training of the personnel of the telecom cadre. For some reason, the initial training of our personnel was being done at ALTTC Ghaziabad, under the aegis of the DOT. Subsequently, in-house training was being conducted in an ad hoc facility co-located with the Stores Section. When I visited the facility, I was literally shocked. There were no laboratories worth the name, and the classrooms etc., were in a dilapidated condition. I wondered why the training of telecom personnel was not being conducted at the Training Institute in Gurgaon, which had excellent infrastructure and facilities. If nothing else the trainees would have decent accommodation and messing arrangements, which were both minimal in the existing set up. When I proposed that this should be done, there was a lot of opposition from the other officers of Telecom Division, who felt that this would result in loss of control over the specialized training of telecom personnel. Of course, their fears were unfounded. When I discussed the issue with the Joint Secretary (Training), he agreed to provide the administrative support, leaving the technical aspects such as syllabus, course duration, assignment of instructors etc., to the Telecom Division. Fortunately, the proposal was accepted, and before I left RAW, the change had been effected.

One reason for the slow progress in implementation of the projects under Vision 2000 was the shortage of manpower. Out of about 100 posts that were to be filled up by deputation in Phase I, less than half had been filled by the time I left. The top level posts at the level of joint secretary and director were filled, but the most important working level posts at the level of under secretary, remained unfilled. When I raised the issue during a conference I was informed that they had tried but could not get volunteers from other departments. This was surprising, since officers from other departments, except the Defence Services, got a promotion when they went on deputation. A little further probing revealed that several officers from DOT had agreed to come, but had cried off when they found that it was intended to send them to outstations, to replace Telecom officers who were keen to come to Delhi to handle the Vision projects. Though Government orders strictly laid down that the Vision posts would be filled only through deputation, the Telecom officers found ways and means to circumvent these orders.

I offered to get officers from the Armed Forces to fill the 14 vacancies of under secretaries that were lying vacant. Once this was agreed, I drafted a letter and sent it to Bikaner House, asking them to send it to the concerned officers in the Service. I personally met the Signal Officer-in-Chief and the Military Secretary in Army HQ, both of whom were known to me. Having worked earlier as Deputy Military Secretary (Signals), I was aware that there were a large number of highly qualified lieutenant colonels and majors who could not get further promotion only because they were in low medical category. There were many M Tech and ME qualified officers who wanted to quit, but were not being allowed to go due to the mandatory service limits laid down. I was sure that they would gladly come on deputation, if given the chance. I made similar calls on the Chiefs of Personnel in Naval and Air HQ, both of whom had done the NDC with me. The Navy was facing a severe crunch and expressed its inability to spare officers at this rank. However, the Army and Air Force both agreed to send names as soon as they received the request.

After about a month I spoke to the concerned officers in Army and Air HQ to find out if they had sent the names. I was surprised when they told me that they had not received any communication from the Cabinet Secretariat in this regard. I spoke to the Director (SR), SK Mehrotra, who checked up from his staff and informed me that the letters had been sent to all the addressees that I had indicated. I waited for a week and again spoke to Army and Air HQ. They still had not received the letters. I knew something was fishy. I went to Mehrotra's office and asked him to get fresh letters made out, which I would deliver myself. This was done and within a week both Army and Air HQ had sent the names. I had already visited the office of the Deputy Military Secretary (Signals), Army HQ and gone through the list of available officers, out of which I had short listed the ones I thought would fit the bill. I think almost half of them were M Tech or ME, in various disciplines.

Once we got the names and the dossiers of the concerned officers, I thought that we would now be able to get some good officers to fill the vacancies. However, I had not taken into account the opposition from the officers of the Telecom Division. Unknown to me, K Rajagopalan, the Director (SM), had initiated a proposal to fill the vacancies from within the Telecom cadre, instead of getting officers from outside. The justification given was the stagnation in the Telecom cadre, many of whose officers were on the verge of retirement after having served for several years in the same rank. While it was true that promotions in the Telecom cadre were slow, the solution suggested was highly irregular. Firstly, it would violate Government orders to fill the posts only through deputation. Secondly, the posts were temporary in nature, and sanctioned only for three years. It would benefit only a few officers, at the expense of those who were to succeed them after a few years.

At that time, Amar Bhushan was the Special Secretary (Personnel). The Telecom officers managed to convince him to recommend the proposal and send it to Bikaner House, where it was again put up to the Special Secretary (SR), who was none other than Amar Bhushan. He submitted the case to the Secretary (R), who approved the proposal. The stipulation about the posts being filled up through deputation was waived on the ground that no suitable officers had been found to fill the posts. This, of course, was a blatant lie. Since the names of the Army and Air force officers had been received through Bikaner House, it is strange that they accepted this plea and misled the Secretary. While all this was going on, almost six months had elapsed since the time we had received the names from Army and Air HQ, who were both pressing for a response. Most of the concerned officers had been kept waiting for a decision, and were overdue for posting. The dossiers were returned and the Service HQ informed that the officers were not required. In the event, the vacancies were never filled, since the Department of Personnel and Training turned down the proposal. Thanks to the short-sightedness and vested interests of a few officers of the Telecom cadre, they had lost a golden opportunity to improve their lot. I am quite certain that the induction of the M Tech and ME officers would have resulted in a qualitative improvement in the performance of the Telecom Division. Perhaps the fear of being exposed played an important role in the resistance of these officers to the induction of officers from outside.

Having pointed out the shortcomings of the Telecom Division, it is only fair that I should bring out their good points. Most of the personnel, especially at the junior level, were dedicated and highly motivated, even while working under adverse conditions. Some of them had to work long hours in uncomfortable conditions, but they took it stoically, without complaints. Sitting in front of a radio receiver with headphones for several hours each day can become tiresome and boring, but they understood that what they were doing was extremely important, which kept their morale high. By and large, most of them were professionally competent not only in operating the equipment, which was highly sophisticated, but also in carrying out minor repairs. Surprisingly, there was no separate trade or category that carried out repairs and maintenance, and a person who worked as an operator at one station could well be working in the workshop in his next posting.

The personnel of the Telecom Division were aware that most of the intelligence gathered by RAW was from electronic intercepts, and were justifiably·proud of this. However, they felt that they were not treated at par with the personnel in the operational divisions, which were more glamorous and got more attention. The Telecom Division was often given stepmotherly treatment in the matter of accommodation, transport, foreign postings etc, and this rankled the men. About a year before I left, when there was a shortage of accommodation in headquarters, it was decided to shift the Telecom Division to the outskirts of Delhi, where the stores were located. This would be unthinkable in any other organisation, given the importance of communications. Of course, the Telecom Division protested, but their objections were brushed aside. The entire Telecom Division could not be shifted because of lack of adequate space at the new location, but part of it had to move. It was a most ill advised step, which is bound to affect the functioning of the Telecom Division in the years to come.

5

The Case of the VHF/UHF Antenna

During the three and a half odd years that I spent in RAW,
I held the appointment of Joint Secretary (TE/DM), which
involved overseeing the functioning of the Procurement Cell,
which was headed by the Director (TE). After Brigadier Datta's
retirement in March 2002, Sampath Krishna, who was from
the telecom cadre, held the appointment. Under him were
two officers, one of who dealt with satellite related equipment,
while the other with equipment for communications and
terrestrial monitoring. During the period I was there, a large
number of procurements were effected, or initiated. Most of
equipment was highly specialized, and the sources of supply
were limited. It was also expensive. However, I sometimes
felt that the manufacturers were taking us for a ride, since the
prices bore no relation to the actual cost of production. One
type of equipment that fell into this category was aerials, or
antennae. In the Army we had often used improvised aerials
fabricated in our own unit workshops. Amateur radio operators,
commonly known as HAMs, usually design and construct their
own aerials. With these, they are able to communicate over

long distances, using sets with very little power outputs. It therefore seemed preposterous to pay lacs of rupees for an antenna that we knew should not have cost the manufacturer more than a few thousand rupees to produce. Of course, the manufacturer always claimed that the major share of the cost incurred by him was in research and development i.e. the design, but this argument did not appear to be very convincing.

Sometime during the last week of July 2002, a file of the Procurement Cell landed on my table. It contained an order placed on Rohde and Schwarz Gmbh for the supply of 27 VHF/UHF log periodic directional antennae (LPDAs), covering frequencies from 30 to 3000 MHz. (The HF band covers frequencies from 3 to 30 MHz; VHF band from 30 to 300 MHz and UHF band from 300 to 3000 MHz). The total value of the order was over Rs. four crores, with the cost of each antenna being about 15.5 lacs. The order had been signed by SK Mehrotra, Director (R) in the Cabinet Secretariat, and a copy had been sent to the Director (TE), who had put it up to me for information. Along with this file, there was another file of the Procurement Cell, which dealt with upgrading of certain monitoring stations. This contained approval of the Secretary for purchase of several items of equipment, including a dozen odd VHF/UHF antennae of exactly the same type that had been ordered from Rohde and Schwarz. However, there was a substantial difference in the price, which had been mentioned as Rs. 2.5 lacs per antenna against Rs. 15.5 lacs being paid to Rohde and Schwarz.

I was surprised at the huge difference in price, since the indent for both antennae had come from the TM Wing. Over the next few days I spent some time going through the relevant files and queried the concerned officers in the Procurement Cell. The order for 27 antennae placed on Rohde and Schwarz covered three different demands for which the Secretary had accorded three different administrative approvals. The first approval was accorded in June 2000 for purchase of 11 antennae at a unit price of Rs. 2.5 lacs; the second approval for 15 antennae was accorded a month later for a unit price of Rs. 4.2 lacs; the third approval for a single antennae was accorded in May 2001 for Rs. 5.5 lacs. The specifications for all were exactly the same and so was the indentor (TM Wing). Why were there such large differences in the budgetary estimates, which were obtained at almost the same time? Even if one took the budgetary estimates as correct, the average price for the 27 antennae would work out to around Rs. 3.5 lacs. Why were we buying them at Rs. 15.5 lacs a piece?

I decided to surf the Internet and find out if the prices were realistic. After browsing the sites of several antennae manufacturers, I found that no one made antennae covering both the VHF and UHF bands completely. The common band covered by most was 30 to 1300 MHz, which was the band commonly being used for communications. If additional coverage was required, a combination of two antennae had to be used. I found that the order placed on Rohde and Schwarz also specified two antennae, which were to be used in combination. The cost of the antennae covering 25 to 1000 MHz was about Rs. 9.6 lacs, while the second one covering 400 to 3000 MHz was about Rs. 1.8 lacs. Hence the cost of the antennae elements alone was Rs. 11.4 lacs. The remaining items such as RF cable, antenna selector, mast and the rotating mechanism etc., accounted for the balance Rs. 4 lacs. On the Internet, the price of the antennae covering up to 1300 MHz was around 300 US $, which worked out to less than Rs. 15,000. In other words, we were paying Rohde and Schwarz almost hundred times what it was costing in the international market.

As I delved deeper into the case, more surprises came to the fore. The first mistake had been committed by the indenting unit, which in this case was the TM Wing. There was no valid reason for the huge difference in the budgetary quotes for the three different demands, at almost the same time. The decision to increase the frequency coverage to 3000 MHz also appeared unjustified, since the antennae that were to be replaced were for frequencies up to 1300 MHz. I found that a year earlier, 34 VHF/UHF receivers had been purchased from Rohde and Schwarz, where a similar increase in frequency coverage had increased the cost by about 60%. Since most well-known manufacturers did not make receivers in this range, very few responded to the tender enquiries. The same thing had happened in the case of the antennae covering the range up to 3000 MHz. Out of 15 firms to whom enquiries were sent, only five responded, and out of these, only two were short-listed after technical evaluation. I had a feeling that the specifications were changed for reasons that were not purely technical.

The second mistake was clubbing three different demands for which three different administrative approvals had been accorded, at considerably different prices. I was told that this was done with a view to reduce paperwork and get a better deal from the vendors, who were more amenable to give a larger discount if the size of the order were large. Even if this was true, the administrative approvals should have been revised, before processing the case further. In any case, the indenting unit should have been asked to explain the reasons for the wide variation in the budgetary quotes, which were all obtained from the same source – Rohde and Schwarz. This was done neither by the Procurement Cell in RAW, nor the Purchase Cell in Bikaner House.

However, the most crucial question still remained unanswered. How was the order placed for Rs 15.5 lacs a piece when the approvals were for prices ranging from Rs. 2.5 to 5.5 lacs? The final price is decided by the Price Negotiation Committee (PNC), which also functions as the Tender Acceptance Committee (TAC). According to the guidelines, the final price cannot exceed the approved price by more than 10%, and in such cases revised administrative approvals have to be obtained. In this particular case, the PNC-TAC comprised Mr. Amar Bhushan, Special Secretary

(SR); Mr. RL Verma, Joint Secretary (TM); Mr. RR Mannan, Director (TM); Mrs. Veena Prasad, Director (Finance); Mr. SK Mehrotra, Director (R) and Mr. Gaurav Sharma, Assistant Director (Purchase Cell). As a rule, officers from the user or indenting unit who are members of the Technical Evaluation Committee (TEC) are excluded from the PNC. However, in this case, both Verma and Mannan from the TM Wing, who had been members of the TEC, were included in the PNC. There was no representative of the Procurement Cell.

The first meeting of the PNC-TAC was held sometime in January 2001, though the financial bids had been opened in September 2000. The price quoted by Rohde and Schwarz, which was the lowest bidder was about 11 lacs for the antenna covering 25 to 1300 MHz and Rs. 2 lacs for the antenna covering 400 to 3000 MHz. The total value of the order was Rs 4.7 crores. The Finance representative, Mrs. Veena Prasad, suggested re-tendering for two reasons. First, she felt that the price was too high. Secondly, the bids had been opened almost three months earlier, which was highly irregular. This was contested by the user representatives, Mr. Verma and Mr. Mannan, who said that the item was urgently required and they were not ready to accept any delay. On the grounds of operational necessity, the Finance representative was overruled. (She later confessed that she had just joined the organization, and this was the first PNC she was attending. She did not want to take a stand, as she was not familiar with the functioning of RAW, and the urgency of its operational requirements. But she found her feet very soon. In subsequent PNCs I found she stood her ground). However, the PNC agreed to ask the firm to reduce the price, which was much higher than the previous procurements, carried out in 1997. Surprisingly, the Assistant Director (Purchase Cell), who was the secretary of the PNC, made no mention of the fact that the administrative approvals were for prices ranging from Rs. 2.5 to 5.5 lacs in the brief that he prepared for the meeting and neither did any member ask for this information.

The PNC met again after about a month, to consider the revised bids of Rohde and Schwarz. The Chairman, Mr Amar Bhushan, did not attend the meeting. After a lot of 'hard bargaining' Rohde and Schwarz agreed to give a discount of 10%, which the PNC-TAC thought was adequate. Once again, there was no mention of the prices approved by the Secretary while granting administrative approval. The minutes were recorded and put up to the Secretary, and his formal approval obtained for purchasing the antennae from Rohde and Schwarz. The Secretary was not informed that the item was being purchased at prices much higher than what he had approved.

Once I had collected the above facts, I decided to bring it to the notice of my superiors. The previous Adviser, Dr. VK Singh had left, and his job was temporarily being looked after by one of the additional secretaries, Mr Rishpal Singh. When he was not present, I dealt directly with Mr CD Sahay, Special Secretary (West), on important issues. After I had put everything down in writing, I rang up Mr Sahay and asked if I could come over. I handed over the note that I had prepared and as he read through it I could see his eyebrows rising. "This is day light robbery", he exclaimed, after he had read through the note. In front of me, he made a few calls. The first was to the Director of Accounts, Mr Baljeet Singh, with a request not to open the LC (Letter of Credit). He then spoke to Mr Amar Bhushan and told that he was sending the note to him. He could examine the issues raised and then decide how the order could be cancelled. I came away from Mr. Sahay's office with the feeling that my efforts had not been in vain.

I also sent a note to Director (R), in reply to his communication under which a copy of the order placed on Rohde and Schwarz had been sent to the Procurement Cell. The anomalies in the entire procurement process, including the PNC-TAC were pointed out, and a request was made to cancel the order. As expected, I received a reply that the order could not be cancelled since all procedures had been correctly followed. Moreover, cancelling the order would have legal implications. Once I realized that Bikaner House had no intention of cancelling the order, I decided that this should be brought to the notice of the 'Chief'. I wrote a demi-official letter to the Secretary, Mr Vikram Sood, giving details of the entire case. I recommended that the order placed on Rohde and Schwarz should be cancelled and fresh tenders floated after a review of the need, numbers and specifications of the antennae. I also recommended that the case should be investigated, along with earlier orders placed on Rohde and Schwarz. I followed this up with a formal note to the Secretary, in which I expressed my fears of the possibility of financial impropriety and misconduct, and the apparent nexus between the company and certain officials of our department, which needed to be investigated.

The last recommendation was based on certain facts that had come to my notice. I had asked the Procurement Cell to compile data of all purchases above Rs. 50 lacs during the last five years. The results were revealing. TM Wing had made six large purchases, totaling more than Rs. 28 crores since 1996-97. Out of these four orders were placed on Rohde and Schwarz, their value being Rs. 23 crores. In other words, more than 80% of the expenditure incurred by TM Wing had benefited one company - Rohde and Schwarz. There appeared to be no doubt about the German company being the favourite, if not the favoured, supplier of TM Wing. During the same period, the SM Wing had placed 10 orders, totaling Rs. 54 crores, each one on a different vendor. In addition, two orders for communication equipment totaling Rs. 2 crores had been placed on two different vendors.

Some other interesting features had also came to light. In the recent past, TM Wing had made two large purchases from Rohde and Schwarz. Microwave equipment costing about Rs. 4.5 crores had been procured in 2001 and VHF/UHF receivers costing almost Rs. 11 crores in 2002. The microwave equipment had not been functioning since its arrival. The company, when contacted, said that our personnel were not properly trained to handle the equipment! This was strange, since six officers had been trained for 12 days in the company's factory in Munich, before the equipment was shipped. I discovered the reason – none of the six was positioned where the equipment was deployed, in a relatively inhospitable place. The case of the VHF/UHF receivers was even more intriguing. The team that went to Munich to carry out the Factory Acceptance Test (FAT) could not complete all the tests and returned after five days. The company later sent the documents to India, and these were signed by the team, comprising Mr. RL Verma, Joint Secretary (TM) and Mr. RR Mannan, Director (TM). Incidentally, Mr. Verma had also conducted the FAT for the microwave receivers, which were found to be non-functional.

While examining the purchases made earlier, I found similar inconsistencies in the purchase of VHF/UHF receivers from Rohde and Schwarz. In almost every case, the price finally paid was much higher than the estimated price for which approval had been granted. In 1994, approval was granted for purchase of four receivers covering the frequency band 30-1000 MHz at a unit cost of Rs. 25 lacs. When the equipment was finally delivered in 1999, the price had jumped to Rs. 43.6 lacs, an increase of 75%. In the year 2000, approval was granted for the purchase of 10 receivers covering the band 20-3000 MHz, the estimated unit price being Rs. 22.5 lacs. The equipment was delivered two years later, the final price being Rs. 38.7 lacs, which was 72% higher than the approved price. Interestingly, 24 additional receivers, with exactly the same configuration, were purchased at the same time, at a unit price of Rs 29 lacs. The PNC for both purchases was held on the same date. There was no explanation for the difference of almost Rs 10 lacs in the unit price of the two purchases, for similar equipment.

Coming back to the antennae, I came to know that my note sent to Mr Amar Bhushan had been passed on to the

Director (R), Mr SK Mehrotra for comments. He prepared an exhaustive note justifying the purchase, and recommended that the order should not be cancelled. This was endorsed by Mr. Amar Bhushan and forwarded to Mr CD Sahay who put it up to Mr Vikram Sood. The Secretary felt that the reasons offered for the high price being paid to Rohde and Schwarz were not convincing, and ordered that the order should be put on hold. He also asked that data be collected on similar equipment purchased by other agencies such as the Army, IB, ARC, Police and the Central Monitoring Organisation. As a result, Rohde and Schwarz were informed that the order was being 'put on hold'. I was asked to obtain the data from other organizations, for the information of the Secretary.

I wrote to the Directorate General of Signals, Army HQ; the Additional Director General of Signals Intelligence, Army HQ; the Intelligence Bureau; the Director, Central Monitoring Organisation, Ministry Of Defence; the Wireless Adviser to the Government of India; the Director Communication, Border Security Force; and the Aviation Research Centre. These letters were all addressed to the concerned officers by name, and followed up with telephone calls. I forwarded the specifications of the antennae we were interested in buying, and requested them to let us know the source and the price, in case they had procured similar antennae earlier. Within a month I had the required information

First of all, no other agency had procured antennae with the frequency range up to 3000 MHz. All antennae procured by them so far were only up to 1300 MHz. This only reinforced my impression that the increase from 1300 to 3000 MHz in our specifications was unnecessary, and had been introduced only to knock other companies out of contention. It transpired that only the Army had procured VHF/UHF antennae in the recent past. The Additional Director General of Signals Intelligence had procured the antennae covering 80-1300 MHz (horizontal polarization) for Rs. 2.5 lacs from Rohde and Schwarz. This was in line with the budgetary estimate for the procurement of 15 antennae that had been obtained by TM Wing in the year 2000. They had also purchased a cross polarized version of the same antenna, which comprised one horizontal and a vertical element, for Rs. 5.6 lacs.

The electronic warfare units of the Army had purchased cross-polarized VHF/UHF antennae from Kaptel Overseas, an Indian firm, for Rs. 61,000 only. I made some enquiries and came to know that Kaptel Overseas was a new company started by a retired commodore of the Indian Navy. I spoke to him on telephone and got the details of the antennae being supplied by him. He told me that the antenna Model CLP 5130/3100 was being imported by them from Create Design Corporation, in Japan. Incidentally, this was one of the firms that I had listed in my note to Mr. CD Sahay. The price I had obtained on the Internet was 300 US $, and when I queried Kaptel on this point they confirmed that this was the correct price, excluding shipping. The price of Rs. 61,000 included Rs. 18,000 each as the cost of the horizontal and vertical elements of the cross-polarized antenna, and Rs. 25,000 for the rotator mechanism. When I asked him if they could provide us cross polarized antenna with the frequency coverage up to 3000 MHz, he confirmed, after a few days, that they could make one for us on order. The additional antenna covering the range from 1000 MHz to 3000 MHz would cost Rs. 72,000. Hence the total cost of the antenna would be Rs. 1.33 lacs. This was less than one fourth of the price that another branch of the Army - Signals Intelligence – had paid for an antenna with lesser frequency coverage, and less than one tenth of the price we were paying to Rohde and Schwarz, for antennae with exactly the same configuration. Obviously, Rohde and Schwarz was the favoured company not only of RAW but also of Signals Intelligence. Perhaps the age of the organizations played an important role. Both RAW and SI were old organizations, with 30-40 years of experience in purchasing equipment. EW units were new to the game, having been raised only in the eighties. Even after that, for the first 15-20 years of their existence they continued using only the equipment of East European origin with which they had been raised, followed by a spell of dependence on the DRDO and PSUs. It was only recently that they had begun to look at private industry for their needs.

I forwarded the above information to Bikaner House, with a recommendation that we should re-tender, including Kaptel Overseas in the list of vendors. At the same time, Rohde and Schwarz had been pestering all and sundry about the order being put on hold, which they said was 'unprecedented'. They held several meetings with the concerned officers in Bikaner House, and sent a number of letters, which were put up with recommendations that we should go ahead and purchase the equipment, since all procedures had been correctly followed. In August 2003 Rohde and Schwarz sent a strongly worded letter, threatening to resort to legal action to claim damages of about 27 million Euros i.e. about Rs. 130 crores. This naturally sent Bikaner House into a tizzy, and they promptly called the company's representatives for a meeting. I attended the meeting held in Bikaner House on 29 September 2003, which was chaired by Mr. Ajay Singh, who had recently taken over as Additional Secretary (SR). Before the meeting, I had briefed him about the case. I had also consulted some friends in the Ministry of Defence and Army HQ on the likelihood of legal action by the company. All of them scoffed at the perceived threat. The general consensus was that if Rohde and Schwarz did resort to legal action, they would soon become *persona-non-grata*, and no government agency would touch them with a barge pole. Obviously, no company would kill the goose that was laying golden eggs. Hence the fears of Bikaner House appeared to be unfounded, and their reluctance to cancel the order appeared to based on other considerations. During the meeting, which I attended along with several others, I asked the representatives from Rohde and Schwarz why they were asking us to pay a price that was much higher than what they had charged from the

Army. They could not give a satisfactory answer, except that they had to manufacture the required items for us as a special case, since they had stopped production of these antennae long ago, and this resulted in additional cost. The meeting proved inconclusive, but I did get the impression that Bikaner House was reluctant to cancel the contract, and the fear of legal action was haunting them.

My recommendation to re-tender was not accepted by Bikaner House. Kaptel's credentials were questioned, since it was an 'untried' company, and there was no guarantee that their equipment would perform well. TM Wing, when asked to justify the increase the frequency coverage, had little to offer except that they had already procured receivers with the higher coverage, and these would not be fully utilised unless the antennae were matching. Of course, there was no confirmed information of our adversaries using the higher frequencies. The Army (Signals Intelligence and Electronic Warfare) units would certainly have procured equipment with higher frequency coverage if they had felt a need for it. Also, the manufacturers would have begun production of the antennae with higher coverage if there was a market for them. Meanwhile, TM Wing had agreed to scale down their demands for the antennae with coverage up to 3000 MHz to nine. Finally, in December 2003 Rohde and Schwarz were asked to deliver only 9 antennae instead of 27 that had been ordered earlier. There was no change in the price, which in fact was now higher, due to devaluation of the Rupee against the Euro. Naturally, the company protested vehemently, and insisted that all 27 must be bought, as ordered earlier.

When I left RAW in June 2004, the case was still hanging fire. However, I have learned that all 27 antennae were eventually purchased. I am not sure if all of them are being put to use. Even if they are, there is no doubt in my mind that public money has been squandered, and Rohde and Schwarz have made a neat profit in the bargain. I am equally sure that this could not happened without the active support of officers in the Telecom Division of RAW and the Purchase Cell in the Cabinet Secretariat. Unfortunately, the organization is not subject to statutory audit by the Comptroller and Auditor General of India. If it was, perhaps this particular expenditure, along with several others, would have caught their eye, and been the subject of a parliamentary question.

6

The VSAT Project

One of the important communication projects that I handled during my assignment with RAW was the Very Small Aperture Terminal (VSAT) satellite project. When I joined the organisation, the existing communication arrangements appeared to be woefully inadequate. While it was possible to exchange telegraph messages, the only method of conversing with officers in other stations was by STD, using the common user circuits provided by the Department of Telecom (DOT), which succeeded the Department of Posts and Telegraphs (P&T). The Telegraph Act of 1885 forbade other agencies from having their own telephone and telegraph lines, which had to be hired form the DOT. Until very recently, even the Army had to depend on the DOT for its static communication network, and it was only in forward areas that it could construct its own cable routes. However, this did not apply to other means of communication, such as radio. During the last two or three decades, the Army had deployed extensive communication networks based on microwave, troposcatter and satellite based systems. These not only provided greater bandwidth, enabling a large number of users to talk at the same time, but were also secure, since they used bulk encryption devices. RAW did have a radio network, but this was used only for passing wireless telegraphy (WT) traffic, which had to be enciphered. Radio telephony (RT), i.e. voice communication was not possible, due to lack of secrecy devices.

A VSAT communication network consisting of 20 terminals had been planned, and partly executed. However, this was totally inadequate to meet the requirements of the organisation. Firstly, it catered only for low speed data, with no voice, and consequently no facsimile (FAX). The data rate was abysmally low (2.8 Kbps), severely restricting its capacity for handling high volume traffic. There was no secrecy device being used, and messages would have to be manually enciphered before transmission and deciphered at the receiving end, as was being done at present. Though only four terminals had been installed, orders had already been placed for 20 on Indian Satellite Limited (ISL), the company that was installing the network. In fact, the product was obsolescent, and a technical journal revealed that during the previous year the company had sold only 20 terminals. In other words, RAW was the only customer of the company's VSATs.

Sometime in April or May 2001, I submitted a proposal for a VSAT network for RAW, which would provide interconnectivity to all outstations. I had seen the benefits of the VSATs used by the Army during my previous tenure in Western Command, especially during the Kargil operations in 1999. The proposal was submitted to the Secretary who directed that I should give a presentation on the subject. In June 2001, I gave a presentation that was attended by all officers of the rank of joint secretary and above, as well as several directors, deputy secretaries and under secretaries from concerned divisions such as Telecom and Crypto. Realising that most officers in RAW were not conversant with the various means of communication and their applications, I decided to spend some time on educating them on these aspects. I went through all the existing methods and means of communication, including line, radio, optical fibre cable, troposcatter, satellite, etc. In radio, bands such as HF, VHF and microwaves were explained, with their applications. The advantages and disadvantages of each were brought out, especially with regard to security, traffic handling capacity, cost, manpower requirements and susceptibility to interference, both natural and manmade. I then suggested a communication policy for RAW, which had not been formulated earlier. In consonance with this policy, I recommended the communication philosophy, for the long term as well as short term. This included a mix of line, radio and satellite, which would cater for our needs, and also provide the required redundancy and security.

The VSAT network was proposed to be established in two phases. In the first phase, a hub with about 100 terminals would be installed. This would provide secure voice and high speed data (64 Kbps), between the headquarters and important outstations. In the second phase, the network would be upgraded from 64 to 256 Kbps and expanded from 110 to 250 stations. The cost of the first phase was approximately Rs 20 crores, which had already been catered for in the Vision 2000 Project. The estimated time plan for the commissioning of the project was one year, from the date the order was placed, which I thought we should be able to do in another year's time. I was way off the mark in my estimations, as I later found.

After a detailed discussion, the Secretary approved the VSAT project. He also approved the communication policy and the communication philosophy that had been recommended. Subsequently, these were submitted on file and formally approved by the Secretary. Brigadier Yugesh Bhardwaj was designated Director (Satcom) and appointed the Mission Officer. He was to be assisted by the Deputy Secretary (Satcom), Mr R Bandhopadyay. Bhardwaj had served with me earlier, as a company commander when I was commanding a mechanised divisional signal regiment. His last appointment in the Army was the Chief Signal Officer of the

Srinagar based 15 Corps, where he had used VSATs extensively. Bandhopadyay was from the Police Wireless, which had recently placed orders for a VSAT network. In the event, the choice of both officers was providential. Both of them performed with rare dedication and industry, and if the project was delayed, it was certainly not because of them.

The first requirement was to make out the draft Request for Proposal (RFP), which constituted the technical requirements that would be sent to the prospective vendors. We had to decide the configuration, which could be Star or Mesh, or a hybrid network comprising both. The access scheme also had to be decided, the choice being DAMA (Demand Assignment Multiple Access), SCPC (Single Channel per Carrier) or TDM/TDMA (Time Division Multiplexing/Time Division Multiple Access). Before finalising the RFP, we decided to carry out an informal survey of the products of various companies in the market. Accordingly, the next few months were spent in visiting establishments or departments that were already using VSAT networks. Some vendors were requested to give presentations of their products, in our office or in their premises. At the same time, we asked all branches within the department to indicate their requirement at each location, in terms of number of users who would need voice, Fax and data terminals.

Bhardwaj and Bandhopadhyaya spent long hours in formulating the draft RFP, which was then sent to the TAG (technical advisory group) for vetting. After the RFP had been approved by the Adviser (Tele), it was sent to the Procurement Cell in Bikaner House along with the list of likely suppliers. The RFP was sent to about 20 companies, which included the well known PSUs such as BEL and ITI as well as private companies such as HCL, Essel Shyam and Bharti. The companies were asked to send the technical and financial bids, in separate sealed envelopes.

A TEC (Technical Evaluation Committee) was constituted to examine the technical bids. I was nominated as the

Chairman of the TEC, the other members being Brigadier Bhardwaj and Mr. Bandhopadhyaya; Mr.K Radhakrishnan, Under Secretary (TAG), Mr. SA Kumar, Director (DM) and Mr. Anjanyelu, Deputy Secretary (Crypto). It was decided to request experts from other agencies to nominate members to the TEC. The outside members were Mr. Kamalesh Deka, Director Police Wireless and IG (communication) BSF; Mr. VK Mittal, from the SAG (System Analysis Group); one officer each from the Signals Intelligence and the Directorate of System Applications in Army HQ. I think this was the first time in RAW that such a broad-based TEC with so many external members had been constituted.

After receiving the tender enquiry, some of the companies asked for clarifications. The queries were received by the Purchase Cell in Bikaner House, which forwarded them to the Procurement Cell in RAW, which sent them to the Mission Officer. The replies followed the same route, in reverse. This naturally resulted in delays, and after a lot of cajoling we were able to convince everyone that the time could be cut down if the Mission Officer could correspond directly with Bikaner House, keeping the Procurement Cell informed. The issue of clarifications necessitated the postponement of the last date of submission of the tender several times. It was only by the middle of 2002 that the companies were able to submit their bids.

Bids were received from 14 companies, which included several government owned PSUs (public sector undertakings). One of the important components of the network was the security system, which very few companies in India were making at that time. The VSAT network installed by the Army a couple of years earlier had a security system made by ITI (Indian Telephone Industries), a government owned company. The other major PSU that had the capability was BEL (Bharat Electronics Ltd). The only private sector company that clai~ to be making security related equipment wa~ Communications. On going through the technical ⸜

found that all companies that had bid for the project were using security systems made by either BEL or Shoghi. In spite of its expertise and capability in the field, ITI had not offered a security system for the project, even in their own tender.

The technical bids were evaluated during the months of July and August 2002. Each company was allotted a day to present and demonstrate its product before the TEC. Wherever the TEC felt that the information was incomplete or needed clarifications, it asked the company to repeat the demonstration, after rectifying the lacunae. Most of these deliberations were conducted in Delhi, Gurgaon or Ghaziabad, at the premises of the vendors. We also visited the ITI factory at Bangalore, to see the facilities available and the products already in the pipeline. However, ITI did not agree to make a new security system for our VSAT project. They did not want to spend time and money on a new system unless they were assured that they would get the order. They felt that their credentials were already established, and they saw no need to demonstrate the security system before they received a firm order.

The TEC must have met about 20 times if not more before it was satisfied with what was being offered. After having deliberated at length, it found that only six vendors were meeting all the technical requirements listed in the RFP. However, before the TEC could submit its report, a new problem cropped up. Mr. RN Mittal, from the DRDO, met the Special Secretary (SR), Mr Amar Bhushan and told him that he had heard that the product of Shoghi Communications had been compromised. Our meetings were usually held in Bikaner House, where Mr Amar Bhushan had his office. After meeting him, Mittal came to the room where the TEC was meeting and repeated what he had told the Special Secretary (SR). Mittal had come to RAW on deputation from the SAG, which was a DRDO establishment located in Metcalfe House in Delhi. He had subsequently asked for reversion to SAG, as he was planning to join the NTRO, which was likely to be raised shortly. Since the rules did not permit moving from deputation to deputation, he went back to 'cool off', so that he could be considered for new organisation. The Adviser (Tele), Dr VK Singh, had also been reverted to Doordarshan, probably for the same reason. Ultimately, both of them joined the NTRO when it was raised a short while later.

Other than the news from Mittal, we had no information about the Shoghi system being compromised, and took it to be a red herring, which it was. Until then, there was no official stipulation of having an indigenous security system, so we saw no reason to react and continued with the TEC. However, in September 2002, a communication was received from Bikaner House, advising that only indigenous security systems were to be purchased for the VSAT network. This literally threw a spanner in the works. Bhardwaj and I met the Special Secretary (West), Mr. CD Sahay and pointed out that this would delay the project by at least a year, since the RFP would have to be amended and fresh tenders would have to be called for. Most of the vendors whose offers had been found technically suitable were using the Shoghi security system. This included several government owned companies. If the bids of these companies were to be rejected, the choice would be limited and we may not get the best product.

During our meeting with Mr Sahay, we also brought out that though the equipment being offered by Shoghi was of foreign origin, the algorithms had been specially designed for RAW. This had already been approved by SAG, which was the only body that was authorised to grade security systems in the country. If there were doubts about the system being compromised, SAG would have withdrawn its approval, which it had not. If considered necessary, we could seek a clarification on this point from SAG. Since Mittal was himself part of SAG, it was strange that he had conveyed his views verbally, instead of sending an official communication. It appeared that the rumour – that is what it appeared to be at that time – had been planted by one of the companies which was not using the Shoghi security system. (About a year after I left RAW, an ex Defence Services officer who was earlier a senior executive in Shoghi, confirmed that this was true. However, they were able to 'persuade' the person concerned to keep his mouth shut thereafter).

Though everyone seemed to be convinced that the Shoghi story was only a rumour, nobody wanted to take a risk since the issue concerned security. We were asked to make out a fresh RFP, incorporating the stipulation about the indigenous security system. Instead of sending out a fresh tender, only the six companies whose product had been found technically acceptable were asked to send revised bids. By this time, Shoghi had roped in an Indian scientist, who was earlier with IIT Kanpur. By the time the revised bids were submitted, he had been able to design an indigenous crypto system for the VSAT network. Fresh rounds of technical evaluation were carried out, and by September 2003, the TEC had finalized its report. The list of companies whose products met our specifications remained unchanged. It took more than six months for Bikaner House to convene the PNC, which met in April 2004. After I left RAW in June 2004, I came to know that the contract had been awarded to BEL (Bharat Electronics Lmited), a public sector undertaking. As it turned out, the rejection of Shoghi was fortuitous. The company was later blacklisted, when it was found that it had submitted a forged end user certificate in another deal.

If the VSAT project came through, it was only due to the relentless efforts of the officers connected with the project. Surprisingly, there was tremendous opposition from within the Telecom Division. Soon after the project had been initiated, I presented the proposed system during the annual conference, which is attended by all RAW officers, including those stationed outside Delhi. After the presentation, the subject was thrown open to discussion. I was able to clarify the doubts raised by outstation officers, most of whom appreciated the concept, realizing that at last they would get an efficient communication system. Then, some officers from the Telecom Division raised questions about the need for going in for the VSAT based system. The Director (TM), RR Mannan, voiced the opinion that the existing system we were using was good enough. I pointed out that the forward elements such as the FIPs (Forward Intelligence Posts) had virtually no communications except the low power HF radio set, which was being used to pass messages to the SBx (Special Bureaux) after manual encryption. It could not be used for voice, due to lack of a security system. I also mentioned that during my visits to several SBx and FIPs I had seen our personnel using the radio for voice communication, which was highly irregular. But one really could not blame them since they had no alternative. Mannan was supported by some senior officers who had obviously been briefed by him. However, the Secretary, Mr Vikram Sood ended the discussion, saying that the VSAT project had already been approved and would continue.

Soon after this, during a meeting of the TEB (Technical Evaluation Board) the Director (SM), Mr. K Rajagopalan expressed the view that the VSAT project was not cost effective, and it would be better to go in for a communication system based on OFC (optical fibre cable). I brought out the point that though OFC offered immense advantages in terms of security and bandwidth, it was very expensive. Unlike the Army, which had laid its own OFC in forward areas, we did not have the wherewithal to lay or maintain such a large network. We would perforce have to depend on the OFC network of the DOT (Department of Telecommunications), which had still not reached many remote regions of the country, especially in Jammu and Kashmir and the North East. I reiterated that this aspect had already been examined at the initial stage, before obtaining the approval of the Secretary, and it would be incorrect to re-open the issue again. However, the Special Secretary (West), Mr CD Sahay, who was chairing the meeting, felt that we should examine the issue afresh, and put it up to him on file.

I was very unhappy with this development, as were Bhardwaj and Bandhopadhyay, since we knew that it would only delay the project, apart from resulting in additional work. But we had little choice and I asked Bhardwaj to obtain from the DOT their existing OFC layout and their plans for extending it during the next few years. I also asked him to do a cost analysis of hiring circuits from the DOT, making a comparison with the VSAT system. It took us about a month to get the required data and carry out a detailed analysis. As I had anticipated, almost half of our FIPs were located in areas where the DOT had no OFC at present, and neither did they have any plans to extend it in future. The report was submitted to Mr Sahay, who told us to go ahead with the VSAT project. In the bargain, we had lost a couple of months, on an exercise that we felt was totally infructuous.

However, if we thought that the voices opposing the project had been quietened, we were mistaken. A few months later, a note was received from the Joint Secretary (SA), Mr. Krishan Varma, expressing doubts about the VSAT project. It said that many advanced countries including the USA were reverting to the use of radio, which was comparatively immune from physical destruction by an adversary. The note, which was addressed to the Additional Secretary (Tele), Mr PV Kumar, said that the VSAT project needed to be re-examined in the light of its vulnerability and costs. When I read the note, I literally lost my shirt. The note contained several technical terms that I knew that Krishan Verma could not be familiar with himself. The note had obviously been prepared by an officer from the Telecom Division, who had asked Krishan Varma to sign it. Having realized that their efforts to derail the projects were not succeeding, these officers were now taking recourse to using operational channels to achieve their aim. The Joint Secretary (SA) functioned as the staff officer to the Secretary, and enjoyed tremendous clout. Everything that went to the Secretary passed through him, as did all orders and instructions emanating from the top. This was perhaps the most serious threat that the project had faced so far, and all of us were worried.

After discussing the issue with the officers of the project team and the Additional Secretary (Tele), I submitted a strongly worded note, listing the history of the VSAT project and the several attempts that had been made to sabotage it. I decided that instead of rebutting the points given in the note, we should try a new tactic. I wrote that since the issue had been raised by a person no less than the Joint Secretary (SA), we would give it the attention it deserved. However, the note contained several technical terms, which I confessed we had not been able to comprehend. I requested that the Joint Secretary (SA) may kindly be requested to give a presentation before all officers, so that we could discuss the issues raised by him. Needless to say, nothing more was heard about it.

Another quarter from which we faced some opposition was the Joint Secretary (Crypto), Mr. Prasada Rao. He had retired about a year after I joined but continued to hold the appointment due to his proximity to the seat of power. There was no doubt that he made special efforts to remain close to senior officers, and was frequently found sitting in their offices discussing maters that had little relevance to his job. He was considered so indispensable that he was employed on contract for two years after his retirement. He thus effectively blocked the promotion of his subordinates, and severely eroded their authority, without being accountable. Of course, he continued to occupy his old office, with the blessings of the Special Secretary (Personnel), Mr Amar Bhushan, with whom he was reported to be very close. When we visited the ITI factory in Bangalore to see the security system for the VSAT project, we were informed that it had already been shown to Amar Bhushan and Prasada Rao, who had visited them a few days earlier. Since both of them had nothing to do with the TEC, I wondered what had prompted this clandestine visit.

Prasada Rao had been instrumental in purchasing the desktop encryptor that was being used by various senior officers with their telephones. It was of Swiss origin and had been procured from a foreign vendor at an astronomical price. The equipment had been purchased from secret funds, without going through the normal process of inviting tenders, evaluating technical bids, and price negotiation. Later, when it was intended to purchase some more pieces of the same equipment, a local vendor offered to supply it at half the cost. However, the most worrisome aspect concerned security. Since it had been purchased from a foreign vendor, its security grading was suspect. In fact, when we met Mr. CD Sahay after the bogey about the foreign origin of Shoghi's equipment was raised, I pointed out that the terminal on his table was also foreign.

Though he was not a member of the TEC himself, Prasada Rao sometimes accompanied the officer from Crypto Division who attended the TEC meetings. He asked awkward questions and cast doubts on the security equipment being offered by various companies. It was obvious that the other officers in Crypto Division did not share his views, and made no secret of their dislike for their previous boss. Mercifully, his contract ended before the TEC could complete its deliberations.

Apart from the overt and covert attempts mentioned above, the issue kept on cropping up during various meeting and conferences. I often discussed the matter with the project team, and other officers in the Telecom Division who had come on deputation. We could not fathom the reason for the opposition to the VSAT project, especially from within the Telecom Division. One view was that it stemmed from jealousy, as the officers from the Telecom cadre would be seen in a bad light if deputationists from outside succeeded where they had failed themselves. If this was all, it was perfectly understandable. However, some of us felt that it was possible that certain people wanted the existing system to continue because of vested interests. The total lack of secrecy in the existing radio communications must definitely be to the liking of foreign intelligence agencies, which must be getting a considerable amount of intelligence by intercepting our links. The same applied to the imported desktop security equipment being used at present. The VSAT network would put an end to this gold mine of information. Were there some moles among us?

7

For a Few Pieces of Silver

The Special Protection Group (SPG) was raised after the assassination of Indira Gandhi in 1984. It is modelled on the Secret Service that protects the President of the United States and members of his family. After Rajiv Gandhi's assassination in 1991, SPG cover was extended to ex-prime ministers and their families. Over the years, the SPG has expanded not only in size but also in authority. Today, it calls the shots in all matters concerning security, often overriding the concerns of the other security and intelligence agencies. The SPG has a virtual *carte blanche* in its functioning, and no expense is spared in equipping it with then latest weapons, vehicles and gadgetry. Like RAW, the SPG is part of the Cabinet Secretariat and works directly under the Prime Minister's Office (PMO). Procurement of equipment for the SPG is done by a Purchase Cell, which works under the Secretary (Security) in the Cabinet Secretariat.

In 1989, the SPG procured a 400 MHz communication system from Motorola, through ET&T. Sometime in 1998, the SPG felt the need to upgrade this system, which was on the verge of becoming obsolete. It submitted a proposal to procure a Motorola 800 MHz secure communication system from Arya

Communications & Electronics, New Delhi, from whom they had earlier been procuring their communication equipment on a single tender basis. When the proposal reached the Ministry of Finance in 2000, it advised the SPG to widen its supplier base and break the tradition of sourcing all their procurement from one company on single tender basis. The Ministry suggested that a senior technical committee be constituted with the aim of widening the technical specifications so that other technically suitable competitors to Motorola could also bid for the tender. In May 2001, the SPG forwarded a fresh proposal for the procurement of a Frequency Division Multiple Access (FDMA) 800 MHz Digital Trunking System at an approximate cost of Rs. 22.60 crores. Apparently, the suggestion of constituting a technical committee to draw out the specifications was disregarded. However, the SPG had contacted several companies to explore the various technologies available. Among these was a new technology known as Terrestrial Trunked Radio (TETRA). The SPG finalized its requirements after technical presentations given by two firms, Simoco Telecommunications and Motorola.

In August 2001, the SPG sent out a global tender enquiry for the procurement of the FDMA 800 MHz Digital Trunking System. Out of 13 firms to whom the enquiry was sent, only four responded. These were Motorola India, Gurgaon; Rotax Electronics, New Delhi; 3G Wireless, Bangalore; and Siemens, Gurgaon. Simoco Telecommunications did not bid, alleging that the specifications had been framed in a biased manner, since Motorola was the only company in the world that could comply with all the requirements given in the tender enquiry. Naturally, the SPG denied the allegation, asserting that the specifications had been drawn on the basis of their communication requirements.

A Technical Evaluation Committee (TEC) was constituted to examine the technical bids of these four companies. The TEC was headed by Mr. Sanjeev Dayal, Inspector General (Technical), SPG. The other members were from the Ministries of Civil Aviation, Communication and Defence, in addition to the IB, Police Wireless and RAW. Brigadier SC Anand, who was working under me as director, was nominated to represent RAW in the TEC.

In its first meeting held in November 2001, the TEC decided to drop Siemens, because it felt that the system being offered by them was very large, with 14 base stations covering the whole of Delhi, which were to be linked by 17 microwave links. Their equipment was also heavy and would be difficult to transport and install. Of course, none of these lacunae constituted a technical shortcoming, which could qualify for disqualification. Thereafter, several meetings and technical presentations were held. None of the firms could demonstrate the portable repeaters that were included in the specifications. During its seventh meeting held on 3 June 2002, under the chairmanship of Mr. SK Jain, the new IG (Technical), the TEC decided to drop Rotax Electronics also, on the ground that the firm had not been able to demonstrate the portable repeater with encryption even after being given sufficient time. This was applicable to the other two companies also, but due to some reasons, only Rotax was dropped.

Now there were only two companies in the race, Motorola and 3G. The TEC visited the Delhi Police HQ and the Mumbai Police HQ where the systems being offered by Motorola and 3G were already working. The TEC also visited the offices, factories and service centres of the concerned firms in Gurgaon and Bangalore. After every meeting or visit, Brigadier Anand briefed me about the outcome and latest developments. One of the important requirements of the system was security, with end-to-end encryption. Surprisingly, the strength of the encryption was not specified. However, I asked Anand to ensure that the encryption system should be SAG approved. The Systems Analysis Group (SAG) is a unit of the Defence Research and Development Organisation (DRDO), which is responsible to grade all encryption systems that are used by government agencies. The SAG tests the system and then allots a 'crack resistivity', which roughly indicates the time that would be required to crack the system. This may be in days, weeks, months or even years.

The TEC submitted its report in August 2002. It recommended that the system offered by Motorola was the better of the two, since their radio was more compact, and had more range. Also, it was a larger company, with better after sales service. The TEC felt that 3G being a new company did not have the infrastructure and expertise to install and maintain the system. The recommendations of the TEC violated the guidelines of the Central Vigilance Commission (CVC), which clearly laid down: "Once it has been established that the offers meet the laid down specifications, the question of 'grading' as well as any 'pick and choose' should not arise. The contract needs to be awarded to the lowest bidder meeting the laid down specifications".

When Brigadier Anand raised the point about SAG approval for the crypto system, the other members felt that this was not necessary. Anand showed them a letter from the Ministry of Defence that stipulated that all crypto systems needed SAG approval, but the TEC felt that since the SPG did not come under the Ministry of Defence they were not bound by these instructions. Anand pointed out that even RAW was not under the Ministry of Defence, but scrupulously followed the guidelines. The SAG was part of the DRDO, which came under the Ministry of Defence, and this was the reason why the latter had issued the instructions, which were to be followed by all government departments. It was only when Anand refused to sign the TEC report that the others agreed to add a sentence at the end: "The firm should submit an appropriate SAG evaluation certificate."

In April 2003 a Tender Acceptance cum Price Negotiation Committee was constituted to consider the financial bid of Motorola for the 800 MHz communication system for the SPG. The chairman of the TAC-PNC was Mr. RN Pandit,

Secretary (Security), Cabinet Secretariat. The other members of the committee were the Additional Secretary & Finance Adviser, Ministry of External Affairs; Joint Secretary (PM), Ministry of Home Affairs; Joint Secretary (Tele), Research & Analysis Wing: Special Commissioner (Communication), Delhi Police; Joint Director, Police Wireless, Ministry of Home Affairs; IG (Technical), SPG; and Director (Security), who was also the convener. Mr. VS Yadav, Joint Secretary (Tele-SM) was nominated to represent RAW in the TAC-PNC.

The first meeting of the TAC-PNC was held on 02 May 2003. Due to some reason, all members could not attend, and the committee was not able to proceed. The second meeting was called on 20 May 2003. Since Mr. Yadav was pre-occupied, I was asked to attend the meeting, which was held in the North Block office of Mr. RN Pandit, Secretary (Security). Mr. Pandit was an ex-emergency commissioned Army officer, who had joined the IAS after completing his term in the Army. He was from the Corps of Signals, which was also my parent arm, and served in 17 Mountain Divisional Signal Regiment, which was also my first unit, though he joined soon after I left. I reached his office a bit early, to reminisce over old times.

Before calling in the representatives of Motorola, the committee deliberated on several points that had been included in the briefing papers, which had been prepared for the members. Since the TEC had recommended only Motorola, the then Secretary (Security), Mr. Y Hari Shanker, had decided that only the financial bid of this company should be opened. This had already been done and the total cost of the equipment was coming to about Rs. 30 crores, which included Rs. 2.34 crores for engineering, training and the factory acceptance tests (FAT) and Rs. 1.4 crores for certain essential operational requirements at the request of SPG. The first point that we discussed was the price. In 1999, Motorola had installed a similar system for the Delhi Police at a cost of Rs. 14 crores, which had been upgraded in 2002 at a cost of Rs. 5 crores. The price of the system being provided to SPG

(Rs. 30 crores) appeared to be very high. The SPG justified the increase in price by saying that the system being procured by them had Over The Air Re-keying (OTAR) facility, which was not there in the Delhi Police system. However, I felt that paying more than Rs. 10 crores for this feature was not really justified.

The next point was cost for engineering, training and the factory acceptance tests (FAT), which was coming to Rs. 2.34 crores. My experience in RAW as well as in the Army was that these services were always provided by the supplier at his cost, and I felt Motorola was not justified in including this as an additional cost. It was also brought out that when the original system had been installed in 1989, the company had not asked for any additional cost on this account. The committee agreed to ask Motorola to waive this cost. Another interesting point was the payment of advance. Motorola was asking for 90% advance payment within 10 days of the contract being signed. I was surprised, since this is the first instance I saw of a company asking for an advance against a government order, and that too such a large amount. Mrs. Veena Prasad, the Finance representative, felt the same way, and it was decided to query the Motorola officials on this point.

It also came to light that a case had been filed by Iridium India against Motorola for fraud and inducement to invest through false claims and suppression of material facts. The Mumbai High Court had issued an interim order restraining Motorola from remitting or transferring any money out of India, until the case was finally decided. A report in this regard had been published in the *Indian Express* dated 19 September 2002. We were surprised at this development, since it could mean that the project could be indefinitely delayed. The committee decided to ask the company to give a clarification on this point.

Once the financial points were over, I asked the SPG officers whether the crypto system being offered had been approved by SAG. The chairman intervened to say that the TAC-PNC was required to discuss only financial aspects, since the technical features had already been examined by the TEC. I clarified that the TEC report clearly mentioned that the company should submit an appropriate SAG evaluation certificate and I was only asking for confirmation if this had been done. At this stage the chairman mentioned that his predecessor, Mr. Y Hari Shanker, had waived the requirement of SAG evaluation, on file. I was literally shocked at this disclosure. The issue concerned the security of a person no less than the Prime Minister, and someone had decided to waive it, just like that!

The officials from Motorola were called. Mr. Ramaakanth Sake, the Regional Manager South-Asia, who had flown down from Singapore for the TAC-PNC, headed the team. He began by informing us that Motorola was providing us with a very sophisticated system not with the intention of making a profit but purely out of a sense of patriotism, since they knew how important it was for the SPG to have the best system available anywhere in the world. I could see that everyone was smiling at his smugness. After a few minutes the chairman asked him to come to the point and we began with the points already listed. When the issue of 90% advance came up, and it was pointed out that no other government department did this, he magnanimously offered to reduce it to 50%, which was what he had got from the Delhi Police. The SPG and Police representatives seemed to be quite satisfied with this. The other points concerning the price, cost of engineering service, training, FAT etc., were discussed, but the company did not yield much. I could make out that they knew that they already had the order in the bag, and that this meeting was a formality.

Finally, I asked them about the security grading of their crypto system. They said that it was very secure, and better than anything that we had. When I asked them to spell out its crack resistivity, I got the same answer, with assurances that it was highly secure. I then asked them if the algorithm for the crypto system had been specially designed or customized for us, or was it the same as the one being used by others. He replied that it was being used in similar Motorola systems elsewhere, but there was no problem, since the keys would be our own. This again was a shocking disclosure, which left me quite disturbed.

Once I returned to my office, I thought over the whole episode, and came to the conclusion that all was not above board. As a rule, security and intelligence agencies always used indigenous crypto systems, with foreign companies only providing the radio system and accessories. Even in the case of indigenous crypto systems, including those developed by public sector companies, the algorithms were customized for the particular agency, and not used by others. In this particular case, the entire set up, including the crypto system, was developed by Motorola, which was an American company. What was especially alarming was the fact that the system was to be used by the SPG, which was responsible for protecting the Prime Minister. The security of the system was definitely doubtful. Since it was being procured from a foreign firm, it was quite likely that foreign intelligence agencies would have access to the algorithm. In other words, a foreign intelligence agency such as the CIA or maybe even the ISI would be able to eavesdrop on the network and know the exact details of the movements of the Prime Minister and the measures being taken to protect him. It was a horrifying prospect. I was reminded of the biblical story, in which Jesus was betrayed by one of his own apostles, for a few pieces of silver.

I discussed the matter with the Additional Secretary (Tele) and told him of my reservations. He agreed that the matter was serious. I told him that I wanted to send an official note to the SPG, voicing my concerns. He asked me to go ahead, giving a reference to the note that had constituted the TAC-PNC. I wrote a note pointing out three lacunae in the procurement process. Of course, the most important was the fact that the crypto system was not indigenous, had not been approved by SAG, and that the algorithm had not been customized for the SPG. The second point was that the SPG appeared to have manipulated the technical evaluation by formulating the specifications in a manner that would result in only Motorola being shortlisted, as had been alleged by another firm. The third point was that the TEC rejected the bids of others without valid reason, and in violation of CVC guidelines. The note was addressed to Mr. JL Sharma, Assistant Director (Purchase Cell), SPG, who had convened the TAC-PNC. I endorsed copies of the note to Mr. RN Pandit, Secretary (Security); Mr. RK Das, Director SPG; and Mrs. Veena Prasad, who was the Finance representative in the TAC-PNC. Mrs. Prasad told me that she would be taking up other points concerning pricing, payment terms etc., through finance channels. I also floated an internal note, for the information of the Secretary, pointing out the above lapses.

I was not sure whether my note would have any impact. I could see that Motorola had very long arms, and it was quite likely that nothing would be done. So I decided, on my own, to inform someone who mattered. Since the issue concerned the Prime Minister's security, I felt that his office must be informed. I wrote a demi official (DO) letter to Mr. PS Raghavan, Joint Secretary (R) in the Prime Minister's Office, apprising him of the lacunae in the crypto system that was being procured for use by the SPG, and the serious implications it might have on the Prime Minister's security.

As I had expected, it was only the DO letter that yielded results. After a few days Mr. Rishpal Singh, who had been promoted as Special secretary, called me to his office. He asked me whether I had written a letter to the Prime Minister's Office. When I said that I had, he asked me why I had not followed the proper channels. I told him that I had already sent a formal note to all concerned officials. The DO letter was in addition to this, and I felt that I had done nothing wrong. We ended the discussion at this point. As expected, the deal was cancelled. After six months, in November 2003 we received a note informing us that it had been decided to constitute a Senior Technical Committee, to firm up the generic specifications for the new communication system to be procured for the SPG, keeping in view the technological changes and the requirements of the SPG. I was nominated as a member of the committee, which did not meet at least for the next seven months i.e. until June 2004, when I retired. (I understand that the SPG finally purchased the Motorola system, without SAG approval. RAW was not consulted, for obvious reasons).

8

The Death of Vipin Handa

The unfortunate accident that resulted in the death of Vipin Handa occurred on 20 March 2003. I was talking to him, and his face was barely six inches away from mine, when it happened. It was one of the most traumatic experiences of my life, and I still shudder whenever I recall it. If the accident had occurred just five seconds earlier, it would have been me, instead of him.

Every Thursday, a conference was held in the conference room on the eleventh floor. All senior officers, in addition to the concerned desk officers, attended it. After the conference, everyone went down to the tearoom on the second floor, for a cup of tea. That day, the conference started at 10 a.m., as usual. It ended at about 11.10 a.m., and we trooped out into the corridor and walked towards the lifts. Out of the six lifts in the lobby, two were normally under maintenance. The lift on the extreme right, towards the conference room, was earmarked for joint secretaries and above. The Secretary and special secretaries usually went down in the first trip, after which the others went down in the second and third trips. Many preferred to use the stairs.

I had not met Vipin Handa before. He had recently returned from Islamabad, after a particularly bad phase in relations between India and Pakistan, which saw almost half the staff of the embassies in New Delhi and Islamabad being sent back. Among those whose tenure was curtailed was Vipin Handa. Being from RAW, he was subjected to severe ill treatment by the ISI, and beaten up several times. These incidents were duly reported in the media, but this did not deter his tormentors. When he came back, his health had deteriorated, and he was a shadow of his former self, according to those who knew him. He was one of the brightest officers in RAW, and highly regarded by everyone. The Islamabad posting was regarded as the most difficult assignment, which had few takers, and this was testimony of his abilities.

After the conference, Handa joined us in the lift for the second trip. There were about 15 of us in the lift, including several additional secretaries and joint secretaries. There were also a couple of directors, including Handa. Being among the last to enter, he was standing near the door, right next to the lift operator and me. After the doors closed, the lift began going down, but suddenly stopped. The operator spoke to the control room on the intercom, and informed them about this. After a few minutes, one of the mechanics opened the doors from outside, with his hands. He informed us that the lift was stuck between the 6th and 7th floors, and that he was going up to switch off the power. The doors then closed again. After about ten minutes, he came down and opened the doors again. He told us that the power had been switched off, and they would try and move the lift manually. The indicator lights had gone off, but went on again. The doors were kept open, as it was becoming stuffy inside. However, everyone was joking, about the coffee getting cold, and that there would be nothing left for us to eat. The others in the tearoom had been told of our predicament, and on his way up to his office, Mr. CD Sahay stopped to ask whether we would like our coffee sent up, since it was taking so long!

After about 15 minutes, someone from outside informed us that it was not possible to move the lift manually, and we should get out. The lift had stopped between the 6th and 7th floors. The opening on top was slightly larger – about 18 inches – than the one at the bottom. This was not the first time I had been stuck in a lift, and had got out either by crawling below the ledge or climbing up to the upper opening, using a stool or another person's back. Fortunately the lift operator's stool was available. Since no one else was ready, I decided to go first. I climbed onto the still, and was pulled up by someone from outside until my stomach was level with the ledge. I turned so that my back was facing outside, and putting both hands on the ledge, pulled myself up so that I was sitting on the ledge. I then swung my legs up from one side, until they were outside, and stood up. The entire operation took barely five seconds.

Vipin Handa followed me. He stood on the stool, and was pulled up by the same person who had helped me get out. I was crouching next to him. I told Handa to turn around, so that he could rest his hands on the ledge, and then pull himself up, as I had done. He had just begun to turn when the lift moved downwards. The top of the lift came to rest on Handa's chest, crushing him against the ledge. He did not utter a sound, and became motionless. His neck and head were outside, facing left, while the lower part of his body was left hanging inside. The gap between the lift and the ledge had been reduced to just about six inches. There were many people standing outside, including some lift operators and personnel from the security and administrative branches. Everyone began scurrying about, trying to get help. I ran down the stairs to the fourth floor lobby, where my PS had her office, and told her to call the doctor from the MI Room, and also inform Control.

Within a few minutes, all the senior officers arrived on the scene. Attempts were made to raise the lift but this did not succeed. After about 30 minutes, people from OTIS, the company that had installed the lift and was responsible for its maintenance, arrived. The fire brigade had also been informed, but they arrived only after an hour or so. Meanwhile, the others who were still inside had to be taken out. They were asked to come out through the gap at the bottom, which had now increased, but having seen what had happened earlier, they were reluctant. However, seeing that there was no other alternative, one by one they came out. Some of them were hysterical, being traumatized by the accident, and the sight of Handa's body, which was still hanging.

Ultimately, some personnel from OTIS went up to the top of the shaft, and were lowered to the roof of the lift. The top of the lift was then dismantled, and it only after this that Handa's body could be removed. It was put in a waiting ambulance and rushed to the hospital. This was several hours after the accident, and we all knew that he had died much earlier, probably immediately after he was crushed. A pall of gloom descended on all of us, and we could do little more than express grief at the loss of life that was totally unnecessary. It was only when one of my colleagues suggested that I should go and offer '*prasad*' in a temple that I realized how narrowly I had escaped death myself. Had the lift moved five seconds earlier, I would have been dead, instead of Vipin Handa.

The matter was reported to the police, who carried out an inquest, since it was an unnatural death. Handa was cremated at Gurgaon. All of us attended the funeral and the '*Chautha*' ceremony that was held on the fourth day. It was heartrending to see his wife and children, who tried to stem their tears. After a few days, the police came and recorded our statements. The Secretary called a meeting of the senior officers, and we felt that the OTIS company must be sued for negligence. They tried to pass it off as an accident and even suggested that someone must have switched on the power. However, I felt that the accident occurred due to faulty design or bad maintenance. There were two questions that no one was able to answer. Firstly, the power had been switched off, and this was obvious to those who were inside also, when the indicators went off. Secondly, the doors were open when the lift moved. Even with the power on, a lift should not move with the doors open. If this were to happen, there would be accidents everyday. Nobody was able to recall a similar incident, when the lift moved with doors open. It was truly a freak accident, which took a precious life.

The death of Vipin Handa was widely reported in the media. Most of the stories were inaccurate, some even absurd. One newspaper reported that his body had been found 'hanging in the' lift, and raised a finger of suspicion against the organization itself. Another felt that the malfunction in the lift was an act of sabotage, carried out at the instance of a foreign intelligence agency. One even speculated that Handa's tenure in Islamabad held the key to the mystery, and felt that the ISI may be behind it. Since I was an eyewitness to the accident, I was amazed and angry at these stories, which had no substance. But I wondered how many of the millions of people who read these newspapers would believe them. I felt that we were ourselves partly to blame, since the media was not given any access or information at all by RAW, and had to concoct such stories. It would have been much better to hold a press conference and tell them what exactly happened, or issue a press release. The armed forces realized the effects of bad publicity several years ago, and put in place a public relations mechanism to counter it. The gains were visible during the Kargil operations in 1999, and convinced even the die-hard critics of the scheme. Regrettably, RAW feels that this would be a threat to their security, and insists on a total ban on any interaction with the media.

9

Signals Intelligence

The primary responsibility of any intelligence agency is collection of intelligence, which falls into two broad divisions – HUMINT (Human Intelligence) and SIGINT (Signals Intelligence). HUMINT relies on intelligence obtained from human sources, verbally or in written form. SIGINT can be further divided into COMINT (Communication Intelligence) and ELINT (Electronic Intelligence). COMINT refers to technical and intelligence information derived from foreign communications by other than the intended recipients. ELINT refers to intelligence derived from non-communications electromagnetic radiations from foreign sources. Another term is IMINT (Imagery Intelligence), in which the source of intelligence is satellite imagery. In day-to-day working, the term SIGINT is often used for intelligence gained from interception of voice, data or facsimile (fax) signals being transmitted by electronic means, as well as through the Internet.

While HUMINT is as old as human civilization, SIGINT became important during the last 100-150 years, after the introduction of the electric telegraph, telephone and wireless. Today, SIGINT has overtaken HUMINT as a source of intelligence, in volume as well as in quality. It is estimated that about 80% of the intelligence collected by most agencies today comes from electronic means, with human sources providing the rest. Paradoxically, the reverse prevails, in terms of resources. This is true even in RAW, where over 90% of the manpower and funds are spent on gaining HUMINT, which probably accounts for less than 10% of the intelligence gained. This was the common refrain of most officers in the Telecom Division, who felt, not without justification, that they were not being given the importance that they deserved.

SIGINT is acquired by intercepting traffic being transmitted through electronic means, which includes physical media or through space. The physical media may consist of lines (terrestrial, underground, or submarine) or OFC (optical fibre cable). Transmission through the ionosphere or space is possible by electromagnetic waves, using various types of equipment, with the transmitters and receivers based on land, sea or air. Electronic interception can be carried out by either physically tapping the physical media, or using another receiver to receive radio signals, without the knowledge of the persons for whom it is meant. Once a transmitter antenna releases electromagnetic waves in the ionosphere or space, any receiver that is tuned to the particular frequency and correctly placed can receive it.

Here, it is important to understand the difference between electronic surveillance, monitoring and interception, though the terms are often used loosely to mean the same thing. Surveillance indicates a continuous round the clock watch over the medium, for a considerable length of time. Monitoring is the term used for observing or keeping a watch on own or friendly transmissions, not for purpose of intelligence but rather for purposes of maintaining discipline, e.g. using the specified bandwidth and power, the correct call signs, breaches of signal security and so on. It is similar to actions of a student monitor who is deputed to look after the other students in the class, when the teacher is not present. Interception is the term used when the link that is being monitored belongs to an adversary or unfriendly agency. By definition, interception is carried out without the knowledge of the legitimate users of the link. The introduction of the Internet has added a new dimension to the concept of interception, since it is increasingly being used not only as a source of information but also a means of communication that is relatively inexpensive, secure and difficult to intercept.

In developed societies, interception of telephone calls and telegraph messages is considered illegal, since it violates an individual's right to privacy. Stringent laws exist to discourage such interception, which is permitted only if the communication is being used for criminal or anti-national purposes. In the case of radio transmissions that can be intercepted off the air, it is impossible to prevent interception. The legal view in such cases, at least in the USA, is that once an individual has broadcast his message through space or an open media such as the Internet, the right to privacy cannot be invoked. In India, there is no legal precedent or ruling on this issue, though the Supreme Court has laid down stringent conditions for intercepting telephone calls.

The USA has enacted the Communication Assistance for Law Enforcement Act, or CALEA, which deals with the interception of digital and other communications. In the UK, there is the Regulation of Investigation Powers (RIP), which regulates the interception of communication by electronic means. Australia has the Telecom (Interception) Legislation Amendment Bill 2000, which regulates interception. Even Russia has the System of Operative and Investigative Procedures (SORM), which deals with interception. Surprisingly, when SORM was introduced in Russia it faced more vehement public opposition than what was seen at the time of enactment of similar legislation in the USA and UK.

In spite of the acts and bills mentioned above, interception is carried out by intelligence and security agencies of almost all countries. The National Security Agency (NSA) in the USA has established a global interception system called ECHELON, which can capture and analyse every telephone call, fax, telex or e-mail sent anywhere in the world. The system is controlled by the NSA, and operated in conjunction with the Government Communications Headquarters (GCHQ) of UK; the Communications Security Establishment (CSE) of Canada; the Australian Defence Security Directorate (DSD) and the General Communications Security Bureau (GCSB) of New Zealand. These agencies work together under the aegis of a secret pact called the UKUSA that was put together in 1948, soon after the end of World War II, mainly to counter the Soviet Union. Though the Cold War is over, the pact and its constituents are active even today.

To carry out its task of global interception, the UKUSA has sub divided the responsibility among its members. The NSA, from its headquarters at Fort George Meade, exercises control over the entire operation. The network relies on inputs from literally hundreds of intercept stations located all round the globe, at military bases or in friendly countries. The main bases for the ECHELON system are Morwenstow and Menwith Hill in the UK; Yakima and Sugar Grove in the USA; Shoal Bay, Bamaga and Geraldton in Australia; Waihopai and Tangimoana in New Zealand; Leitrim in Canada; Bad Aibling in Germany; Misawa in Japan, Diego Garcia in the Indian Ocean and Ascension Islands in the Atlantic. In addition to ground-based stations, there is a network of surveillance satellites that were launched by the NSA in cooperation with the CIA. These satellites pick up almost every radio transmission in their area or coverage, including cell phone conversations. The Menwith Hill facility of the NSA in Yorkshire, England, is said to be the largest spy station in the world, with over 25 satellite receiving stations. About 1,400 American NSA personnel and 350 personnel from Britain man the station.

In the late 1990s, the Federal Bureau of Investigation (FBI) developed the CARNIVORE, a diagnostic tool used for interception of Internet traffic. Approval for use of the

CARNIVORE was given by the US Congress for fighting cyber crime, terrorism, espionage, fraud, child pornography and information warfare. In accordance with the existing US laws, the FBI can intercept Internet traffic emanating from known addresses, after obtaining a court order. The actual interception is carried out by the Internet Service Provider (ISP), to the extent authorised by the court order. A sniffer is used to identify and filter traffic emanating from or going to the specified address, which is then made available to the FBI. To enable CARNIVORE to be used, ISPs are required to provide one-way taps, so that the traffic passing through the hub or switch is not altered or corrupted during the process of sniffing.

From the above, the reader would have got a fair idea of the existing set up in other countries with regard to electronic interception. I will now deal with the subject as it pertains to RAW. As mentioned earlier, terrestrial and satellite monitoring, or interception, were being looked after by the other two joint secretaries, RL Verma and VS Yadav. For obvious reasons, I cannot give details of our facilities, such as their number, location or equipment being used. It would be sufficient to state that our capabilities in these areas were not insignificant and formed the source of the bulk of our intelligence inputs. As Joint Secretary (Tele –TE/DM), data monitoring was part of my duties. There were two officers exclusively responsible for data or Internet monitoring. SA Kumar, the Director (DM), was a soft-spoken but exceptionally bright officer, who shunned limelight. He had come on deputation from the Ministry of Information Technology, where he worked in the ERNET (Education and Research Network). The Deputy Secretary (DM), Pradyumna Kant, who had some experience with computers, assisted Kumar. When I joined RAW in November 2000, expertise on Internet monitoring was virtually non-existent in the country.

Unlike terrestrial and satellite monitoring, which were off the air, Internet monitoring would have to be done by physically tapping or sniffing the communications channel, as was being done in the USA using the CARNIVORE diagnostic tool. However, US laws stipulated that the FBI could use CARNIVORE only after obtaining a court order. Did we need such an authorisation in India? Legislation in India comprised the Indian Telegraph Act, 1885, the Indian Post Office Act 1988, and the Indian Wireless Telegraphy Act 1993, which covered basic telephone and telegraph services and basic wireless services respectively. The Information Technology Act that was enacted in June 2000, dealt only with e-commerce and cyber crime. None of these Acts covered the use of the Internet. In 1997, a Committee of Secretaries had deliberated on the issue and ruled that Internet Services are 'value added services', in accordance with the definition promulgated by the ITU (International Telecommunication Union). A few years earlier, the Supreme Court had given a ruling that delineated the circumstances under which security agencies can be granted permission to intercept telephone calls. The ruling, based on the provisions of the Indian Telegraph Act, specifically talks about 'telephone tapping' and makes no mention of basic services such as postal or wireless. The view in the intelligence and security agencies was that being a value added service, as distinct from basic services such as telephone and telegraph services, interception of Internet was not affected by the Supreme Court ruling. Of course, if someone filed a case in the Supreme Court, it was not improbable that a similar ruling would be handed down for Internet also.

Internet came to India in the nineties. In the beginning, Internet services were provided only by the government owned VSNL (Videsh Sanchar Nigam Limited). On 16 September 1997, the Cabinet Committee on Infrastructure decided that private operators should be permitted to provide Internet services on demand at reasonable rates. It also decided that the backbone for the National Information Infrastructure should be established quickly utilizing the infrastructure available with the DOT, Railways and Powergrid Corporation. To ensure early realisation of the objective of upgrading

Internet facilities in India to global standards, a committee was set up, under the chairmanship of Dr Bimal Jalan, Member Secretary, Planning Commission. The committee submitted its report in a couple of weeks, which was remarkable. On 17 October 1997, exactly a month after its constitution, the Cabinet approved the Jalan Committee's report in toto. However, it directed that the security aspects should be carefully considered and settled after inter-Ministerial consultations and with the concerned security agencies.

In 1998, the Prime Minister constituted the National Task Force on Information Technology and Software Development. Based on the recommendations of this task force, the Government of India formulated the Information Technology Action Plan, which was promulgated in the form of a Gazette Extraordinary. Paragraph 101 of the Action Plan states: "On security related issues an Inter-Ministerial Committee shall be set up consisting of representatives of DOT, Cabinet Secretariat, MHA, MOD, DOE, and NIC and representatives from NASSCOM to look into the technical aspects of monitoring of communications in this sector (including Internet) to enable the setting up of the monitoring infrastructure (which in many cases would have to be funded by the ISPs) and incorporation of suitable clauses in the licence agreements."

The Inter-Ministerial Committee was duly set up and gave its recommendations. One of the important provisions related to the provision of a free port on each router of more than 2 MBPS at ISPs, to facilitate monitoring by intelligence and security agencies. The ISPs were also to bear the cost of the monitoring equipment, which was then estimated at about Rs. 4 lakhs. One member who had serious reservations about these provisions was Dewang Mehta, the president of NASSCOM (National Association of Software and Service Companies). He felt that it was unfair to ask the ISPs to bear the cost of monitoring equipment, and leaving one port on every router would add to their cost. He also expressed his misgivings about the agencies carrying out monitoring without orders from the court or a competent authority, as was being done for interception of telephone calls. On 25 February 1999 Mehta wrote to Mr. N Parmeswaran, Deputy Director (LR), Department of Telecommunications DOT:

> 'I still feel that ISPs not applying for international gateways should not bear the cost of monitoring. On the contrary, to request them to keep one port free on a router of more than 2 MBPS is itself a cost to an ISP, (which I'm uncomfortable with). So to ask for more would only mean increasing the cost to the end user.

> I agree that "in-principle, the security or monitoring agencies should have the ability to monitor, and therefore, we are asking ISPs to keep one port "free" on the router from beginning. This also does not mean that an ISP router should be connected 24 hours to monitoring agency, because then, how do we protect privacy of users? There is a law of the land which allows monitoring agency to monitor subject to court order or through orders from competent authority. So how do we ensure that monitoring agencies will not monitor what they are not supposed to?

> Even for international gateways, as long as it is monitoring of gateway only, I'm OK. But then also, constant monitoring or random monitoring without court orders is a problem. I hope we have a solution to this.

> I strongly feel that the security interests of the country should not be jeopardized, but at the same time, we should not also infringe user's privacy.'

It is not known whether Dewang Mehta's views were given the attention that they deserved. If they were, there was no evidence of it in the final recommendations of the committee. However, an Inter-Ministerial Group was constituted, to screen proposals for establishment of ISPs and Internet gateways from security angle. The group was also to decide on the modalities and mechanism for carrying out monitoring at the ISPs and gateways. RAW was nominated as the nodal agency to coordinate the functioning of the group, which had members from all security agencies, DRDO, C-DOT and DOT. In practice, the meetings were held in the office of N Parmeswaran, Deputy Director General (LR), DOT. From RAW, I attended the meetings, accompanied by SA Kumar and P Kant. Mr. ESL Narsimhan and Mr. BV Wanchoo usually represented the IB. None of the other security agencies attended the meetings. Mr. Chauhan represented C-DOT (Centre for Development of Telematics), while the DRDO was represented by Dr. Sitaram of CAIR (Centre for Artificial Intelligence and Robotics).

The group had met a couple of times before I joined. I found that it had been decided to ask ISPs to deposit a sum of five lakh rupees, which was estimated to be the cost of the computer that would have to be installed for monitoring purpose at each ISP. The responsibility for procuring the computers and installing them was assigned to C-DOT. However, the actual methodology and software for monitoring had still not been decided. Though the software was commercially available in the market, it had been decided to assign the responsibility of developing the monitoring software to the DRDO. A team from CAIR was working on the project, in collaboration with Prof. N Balkrishnan of the IISc (Indian Institute of Science), Bangalore. During 2001 and 2002, there was little progress, though CAIR assured us that the software would be made available soon.

After more than two years, a trial version of the software called NETRA was given to IB and RAW. One computer each was installed at two ISPs, which could be accessed from our location using a password. After several weeks of hit and trial, we were able to commence the trials. We found that the software had several snags, which were brought to the notice of the DRDO and IISc, through the DOT. One day, I received a call from the DOT that the SA to RM (Scientific Adviser to the Raksha Mantri), Dr APJ Abdul Kalam, would be visiting the offices of RAW and IB along with Prof Balkrishnan to see how the software was functioning. Unfortunately, we were having our annual conference that day, and I knew that nobody would be free. Since the SA to RM was coming, he would have to be received by the Secretary, and I was doubtful if I could get him to agree at such short notice. In any case, I told the caller, the software was not working properly and there was little use showing it to Dr. Kalam. When he insisted, I told him that in case he did come, we would tell him in no uncertain terms that the software did not meet our requirements. This naturally resulted in the proposal to visit RAW being dropped.

At the next meeting of the group we were informed that since the software had been installed, we could commence our monitoring operations. The DRDO also presented a bill for the cost of developing the software, which had to be paid by the users, i.e. the security and intelligence agencies. Of course, we contested both proposals. The software was not working, and could not be used until the snags had been removed. Surprisingly, the IB seemed to be very happy with it. When we asked them if they had used it, they confirmed that they had. Later it was revealed that the IB had taken their computer to the ISP itself, and were not using it from a remote location, as was intended. There also seemed to be a difference in opinion among the officers of IB as regards the software. Mr. Narsimhan seemed to find no fault with it, while the others were apparently not very happy with it.

After a couple of weeks I was asked by the Special Secretary (West), Mr. CD Sahay, to accompany him to a meeting of the Committee of Secretaries, being chaired by the Cabinet Secretary. In normal circumstances the Secretary would have attended but since he was away, Sahay was officiating. Before the meeting, he asked me if the software designed by Prof. Balkrishnan was functioning. I replied in the negative. The Secretaries of several other ministries such as Home, Defence and Communications were present in the meeting. In the meeting, the Communications Secretary complimented Prof Balkrishnan on having done designed an excellent job, which would prove to be great help to the security agencies. Prof Balkrishnan presented three gift-wrapped CDs to the Cabinet Secretary, who gave one each to the Communications Secretary and Directors of RAW and IB. When the Cabinet Secretary asked the users if they were happy with the software, the IB answered in the affirmative. When it was the turn of RAW to speak, Mr. Sahay asked me to respond. I brought out the shortcomings that we had noticed, which in any case had been brought to the notice of Prof Balkrishnan as well as the DOT. Prof Balakrishnan responded that these were teething troubles, which would soon be removed. After a few days, I read in the newspapers that Prof N Balkrishnan's name was included in the list of persons who were to be awarded the Padma Shri. The reason for his keenness to bring Dr Kalam to RAW and IB, and Narsimhan's commendation of the software now became clear.

As it happened, it was only in late 2003 that a workable version of the software was given to us by CAIR. In the bargain, we had lost almost four years of precious time. Seeing the project being delayed, both RAW and IB had been exploring other avenues. A number of private companies had demonstrated their products, which could be purchased off the shelf. However, to use the software we had to install the monitoring computers at the ISPs, which could not be done without bringing the other users into the picture. At one stage, we were all so fed up that at the next meeting of the group, it was decided to set a deadline. If the DRDO was unable to give us the software in six months, we would buy it from private sources. It was only after this that the trial software was received.

Soon after this there was an interesting development that gives an insight into the traditional rivalry between RAW and

IB. When the Supreme Court delivered its judgment in the telephone tapping case, it listed seven agencies that could be given permission by the MHA (Ministry of Home Affairs) to intercept telephone calls made from specific numbers for specified periods. Interestingly, RAW was not included in the list, which was submitted to the Court by the MHA. This was probably due to the feeling that since RAW was responsible for external intelligence, it would never have the need to tap the telephones of Indian citizens living in India. Whenever RAW had to tap telephones in other countries it had to be done covertly, with the attendant risks. The other reason, which appeared more plausible, was that since the list was prepared by the MHA, it naturally included only the law enforcement and security agencies that came under its jurisdiction. For this reason, even Military Intelligence was not in the list.

In recent years, the Army had been conducting counter-insurgency and anti-terrorism operations in Jammu and Kashmir, where the anti-national elements were found to be using the Internet for communications. The Army wanted to carry out interception of Internet traffic, but was not given permission, since it was not in the list of agencies that could be allowed to tap telephones. Finally, under great pressure from the Ministry of Defence, the MHA granted permission to the Army (Signals Intelligence) to monitor Internet services in Jammu and Kashmir under the provisions of the Telegraph Act. As already brought out, this was contrary to the view of the Government set out in the report of the Committee of Secretaries in 1997 that Internet was a value added service. Since the Telegraph Act applies only to basic services such as telephone and telegraph, its application to the Internet was obviously incorrect. More interestingly, if the Telegraph Act covers Internet, it would bring it within the ambit of the Supreme Court ruling, effectively debarring all security agencies from monitoring it.

The IB saw a golden opportunity and seized it with both hands. It represented to the MHA that since RAW was not included in the list of seven agencies that could be permitted to intercept telephone calls under the Telegraph Act, it should also be debarred from intercepting Internet traffic. The IB also felt that it should replace RAW as the nodal agency for Internet monitoring, as decided earlier by the Inter-Ministerial Committee. When this was sent to RAW for comments, it threw everyone into a tizzy. Letters were written and meetings were held with officials in the MHA. My own view was that we should ignore it, since the MHA had no authority to decide whether the Telegraph Act covered Internet monitoring or not. The nodal ministry until now had been the Ministry of Communications, which should be approached to clarify the issue. In fact, I suggested that the matter should be taken up with the PMO, which was the correct channel for RAW to represent its case. The Secretary (R) was the only head of an intelligence or security agency with direct access to the Prime Minister. If he could not use this privilege now, when would he use it? In any case, it would be inconceivable for the country's premier intelligence agency to be debarred from a source of intelligence that was available even to smaller players such as the NCB (Narcotics Control Bureau), DRI (Directorate of Revenue Intelligence) and the EOW (Economic Offences Wing) of the Delhi Police. Could one imagine the CIA in USA being told that it could not monitor Internet traffic, while the NYPD (New York Police Department) could do it? In any case, debarring RAW would only harm the overall intelligence effort, instead of helping it. This was another example of the turf war between our intelligence agencies, which continues even today.

With the passage of time, it was realized that the sum of five lakh rupees was insufficient to meet the cost of hardware. It was then decided that all ISPs would in future install the hardware themselves, irrespective of the cost. This was also applicable for ILD (International Long Distance) gateways. Without going into details of the facilities that exist today, it can be said that the Internet is now a major source of intelligence for security and intelligence agencies. The only problem with the Internet is that it has to be intercepted at the ISPs or the gateways. Smart terrorists are now using satellite terminals, with which they directly communicate with an ISP based in the USA, UK or UAE. Since these communications do not use a gateway in India, it is almost impossible to intercept such messages. Of course, the transmissions from the satellite terminal can always be intercepted, if one has the necessary equipment.

Another interesting incident relates to the interception of traffic passing along the SEA-ME-WE (South East Asia-Middle East-Western Europe) cable. The SEA-ME-WE 2 submarine cable connecting Western Europe, Middle East and South East Asia was laid in the late 1980s. Encouraged by the success of the venture, Singapore Telecom and France Telecom started preliminary studies in 1993 for a cable with much higher capacity linking Europe to the Asia-Pacific region. In December 1994, a Memorandum of Understanding was signed by 16 parties for the development of the Sea-Me-We 3 project between Western Europe and Singapore. In November 1996, additional MOU(s) were signed to extend the system from Singapore to the Far East and to Australia. Finally in January 1997, the Construction and Maintenance Agreement for Sea-Me-We 3 was signed by 92 International Carriers. The network was completed by the end of 2000.

Sea-Me-We 3, which is also called SMW 3, has 41 landing points in 35 countries and four continents from Western Europe (including Germany, England and France) to the Far East (including China, Japan and Singapore) and to Australia. Built at a cost of US $ 1.5 billion, it is the longest system in the world with a total length of 39,000 km. Due to the huge capacity (70 Gbps) and excellent connectivity to many countries and its innovative pricing structure, SMW 3 is being used to meet the traffic needs of the new technologies such as broadband services, Internet, video services and ATM (Asynchronous Transfer Mode). The cable has two landing points in India, at Mumbai and Kochi. The system is maintained and upgraded by a consortium of 93 firms, with VSNL the sole Indian member of the consortium.

VSNL, which was earlier known as the OCS (Overseas Communication Service), was a government owned company until it was privatized in 2002-3. The Tata Group now owns it. The ILD (International Long Distance) gateways at Bombay and Kochi are owned and operated by the VSNL. These gateways carry long distance traffic between India and most countries of Western Europe, Middle East and Far East. The bulk of long distance traffic, including audio and video services and Internet, also passes through the gateways. In addition to the SMW, Bharti has laid the i2i cables between Madras and Singapore, in collaboration with Singapore Telecom.

Sometime in 2000-2001, someone in RAW proposed that monitoring equipment should be installed at the VSNL gateway in Mumbai. When I joined RAW in November 2000, the project was still being discussed. I was not directly involved with the project, which was being handled by the Joint Secretary (SM), VS Yadav. However, it was discussed in the regular meetings in the Telecom Division to monitor the progress of various projects. When the project was planned, VSNL was still a government owned company. It agreed to provide the facilities for installation of the interception equipment, but expressed misgivings about the presence of RAW personnel and equipment in its premises, which were frequently visited by foreign members of the consortium. I am sure VSNL must be aware of the Supreme Court's ruling regarding interception of telephone calls, but apparently their fears were allayed by a bit of arm twisting.

The problem of RAW's presence was solved by suggesting to VSNL that the equipment should be purchased by them, with the cost being reimbursed by RAW. After some hiccups, this proposal was accepted by VSNL. However, a new problem arose when the people in Finance refused to clear the payment to VSNL, unless they were given details of the project with full justification. Again, the matter had to be taken up with the Ministry of Finance at a high level, with liberal use of appropriate phrases such as 'national security' and 'urgent necessity'. Even while this was going on the status of VSNL changed, and it became a private company, owned by the Tata Group.

I had felt uneasy about the project right from the beginning. It would have been okay if we were going to intercept traffic going from or coming to India. One could always justify this on the ground that we wanted to monitor traffic related to terrorism, drug trafficking, money laundering, 'hawala' transactions, evasion of taxes and duties and so on. But the SMW3 was also carrying traffic that had nothing to do with India. What right did we have to monitor a call between a person in Germany who was talking to someone in Japan? Apart from our own laws, we had to consider international laws. Would there not be an uproar, resulting in embarrassment to India, if this ever came to light? I was quite sure that the proposal did not have the blessings of the PMO, which would have been well aware of the international ramifications of such an activity.

I expressed my misgivings several times, trying to draw a line between legal interception, such as intercepting radio or satellite traffic off the air, and illegal interception, such as tapping telephones without authorization. What we were planning to do was clearly another form of illegal interception. In fact, it was worse because we would not only be violating our own but also international laws. I was surprised when I found that other people in RAW not only disagreed but scoffed at my ideas. According to them, there was nothing illegal about intercepting international calls. In fact, for RAW, almost all activities connected with acquisition of intelligence abroad were illegal, and if they were to keep this in mind they would not be able to do their job. The CIA routinely carries out such activities and no one should be surprised if RAW does the same thing. In the world of espionage, there are no rules and taking risks is part of the game.

When VSNL was privatized, I thought they would back out of the deal and the problem would be solved. But apparently this did not happen. The management remained unchanged and we continued to deal with the same officers. VSNL desired that a new agreement should be signed with them, and this was done. I am not sure whether details of the project were brought to the notice of the new Chairman or the Board of Directors. In fact, I am not sure if the project was implemented at all, since I left RAW in June 2004. But the fact that it was planned and approved raises many questions. Espionage is a dirty business but an honorable profession. It is difficult to lay down rules that intelligence agencies must follow to acquire intelligence. Spies are fiercely patriotic and take grave risks in carrying out their tasks. It is a pity that most of their exploits remain unknown and unrewarded. However, intelligence agencies need to be reminded, occasionally, that they are working not for themselves but the country and its citizens, who must never be humiliated by their actions.

10

The Rabinder Singh Episode

In the middle of May 2006, the country was rocked by the news that a senior RAW official, suspected to be an American mole, had vanished. For the next few months, the newspapers were full of stories about how Rabinder Singh, then a joint secretary in RAW, had defected with the help of the Americans and possible connivance of some officers within the organisation. There were reports that he had gone to the USA, where most of his family had already moved. However, nobody knew his exact whereabouts, though some newspapers have reported that he lives in Jackson Heights, in New York. The government has not come out with any evidence of his having passed on sensitive information to the people he is alleged to have been working for, in spite of the fact that he was under surveillance for several months before his desertion. However, Rabinder's defection did serve a useful purpose – it exposed the chinks in the counter-intelligence apparatus of the country's external intelligence agency, which hopefully have been plugged.

Rabinder Singh is a clean-shaven Jat Sikh from an affluent landed family of Amritsar. He joined the Army as a commissioned officer, and served in the Gurkhas. While in the Army, he took part in Operation Blue Star, the counter-terrorist assault on the Golden Temple in 1984. Shortly afterwards, he joined RAW on deputation, along with several other officers. On completion of his deputation, he opted for permanent absorption in RAW, where life was probably not as hard as in the Infantry and promotions were faster. He gave up his lien on the Army and became a member of the Research and Analysis Service (RAS). Throughout his career, he was considered by many of his superiors and peers as an average officer. Initially, he was stationed in Amritsar where his principal task was the collection of trans-border HUMINT (human intelligence) about the Pakistani Army and the training of Sikh terrorists by Pakistan's Inter-Services Intelligence (ISI) in Pakistani territory. Subsequently, he was posted to West Asia, where his task involved monitoring the activities of terrorist groups there. He also did a stint in West Europe, where he focused on the activities of Sikh terrorist elements operating in that region.

When I joined RAW in November 2000, Rabinder was in Amsterdam. Soon after I joined, NV Menon, who had just returned from Amsterdam, was assigned to me as my Private Secretary (PS). Menon was a first class PS, and seemed to have high regards for his previous boss. I met Rabinder for the first time only a year later, when he returned to India. Since I was one of the two senior Army officers in the organisation, Rabinder made a courtesy call on me a couple of weeks after his arrival. Thereafter, our spheres of work being dissimilar, we met only at official meetings or social functions. He did call me for dinner once but I had to decline because of another engagement.

In April 2003, I had to go to Japan to attend a seminar. I was accompanied by another officer, who was an under secretary. Since Rabinder was looking after the region, he coordinated all the arrangements for our visit. I had to go to his office a couple of times in connection with our visit. He was very helpful, and went out of his way to see that everything was tied up. The senior RAW officer in Tokyo was not present, but his deputy was told to look after us. He received us at Narita airport when we arrived, and took us to our hotel in a vehicle that he had arranged from the embassy. Of course, he invited us for a meal in his house, as well as once in an Indian restaurant. When we were returning, he asked me if we could carry something back. He gave us two bottles of Black Label scotch whisky which he requested be handed over to Rabinder. I do not know whether Rabinder paid for the whisky. In all probability, it was a gift. I was given to understand that this was customary, and the accepted method of replenishing the cellars of senior officers who had developed a taste for scotch whisky, thanks to their foreign assignments.

Sometime in the middle of April 2004, there was a surprise check of briefcases at closing time, when everyone was leaving for home. I was on leave that day, and came to know of it through my driver, when he came to pick me up next morning. He told me that there was a commotion, since a thing like this had never happened before. Of course, it was normal practice to conduct such surprise checks once or twice a month in several defence establishments, including Army HQ. Perhaps in RAW this had been done for the first time and caused considerable consternation. At the next weekly conference, the Secretary clarified that the checks were not directed at any person in particular but were conducted with the intention of tightening security. Rabinder was present, and when the conference ended, he walked out with the rest of us, muttering loudly that this was not the proper way to treat senior officers. I later found that the whole exercise was for his benefit.

I am not sure if anything incriminating was found in his brief case during the search. Even if it was, there was little that could have been done. In India, senior bureaucrats routinely take files home, in the black 'dak box', a legacy of the British days. It is supposed to be locked, with the key held by the officer himself. Unlike Army establishments, RAW did not have the system of a round the clock duty officer to whom important messages could be delivered outside office hours. Consequently, the common practice was for the signal centre to send even top-secret messages received outside office hours and on holidays to the residences of senior officers. The first time I received such a message, I was aghast. But I was informed that this had been the practice since the time RAW was raised, and nobody saw anything wrong in it. So, even if Rabinder was found taking classified documents home, I don't think much could have been done about it.

It was also reported that he had been photographed making copies of secret documents in his office. Again, this was perfectly normal. Photocopiers had been placed in the offices of senior officers in order to enable them to make copies of sensitive documents themselves, rather than relying on their personal staff. Joint secretaries often received important letters or circulars that needed to be brought to the notice of directors or deputy secretaries. The best way to do this was to make photocopies, which were then sent to the concerned officers under a covering letter. Unless Rabinder was caught handing over these documents to unauthorized personnel, I doubt if he could have been nailed.

Rabinder did not come to the office after this, but this was not unusual. Earlier, another officer who was not promoted from additional secretary to special secretary was so peeved that he just stopped coming to the office. He resumed only after several months, when his promotion came through. So Rabinder's absence did not raise any eyebrows. Then, on 14 May 2004, he just vanished. It was only after reading the newspapers that I came to know of his disappearance. According to the story, he had been put under surveillance after an American diplomat in Delhi dropped his name inadvertently. His telephone calls were monitored and a camera was placed in his office. He was photographed making copies of documents on the photocopier kept in his office. It was only after this that his brief case had been searched. The news story said that Rabinder was an American mole, and had probably gone to the USA, with the help of the Americans.

During the next few days, I heard all sorts of stories about him in the office. The last person to have seen him was his driver, who said that he had dropped him at the railway station to catch a train to Chennai. Obviously, this was done with a view to cover his tracks. There were some who discounted the story about his being a mole, and felt that he had just gone to attend the engagement ceremony of his daughter in the USA. Apparently, he had applied for ex-India leave and permission to go abroad, according to the rules, but this had been refused. This had earlier happened to several other officers, who had to cancel their tickets and make fresh bookings due to the inability of the security staff to process the applications in time. At that time, Amar Bhushan, who was heading the ARC, was also the self-styled Special Secretary (Personnel) in RAW. All applications for visits abroad on leave needed his approval, and since he was rarely available, the applications were usually delayed. Amar Bhushan had a mercurial temperament, and often refused such requests. It was possible that Rabinder had got fed up with the 'babudom' that prevailed in the department, and left in a fit of rage.

The version that appeared most plausible was that Rabinder had gone to Kathmandu, from where he went to the USA on an American passport. Most of his family, including his wife and daughter, were already in the USA. It was said that his sister was an American citizen, who was working for the United States Agency for International Development (USAID), a donor organisation that was suspected to be a front for the CIA. It was also reported that Rabinder had once carried out an operation for the collection of intelligence about US Government activities in South Asia through his sister. Initially, some good information came out of this operation, but subsequently, there was a doubt that the CIA might be using his sister to plant disinformation on the Government of India through him. One such piece of disinformation, which the CIA allegedly tried to feed through this channel in the late 1980s, was that the US embassy in New Delhi had reported to the State Department that the then Chief of the Army Staff was planning a coup against Rajiv Gandhi. Understandably, Rabinder had been under suspicion ever since.

The suspicion against Rabinder was re-inforced when it was found that he had been facing severe financial problems for several years. In 1992-1993, his daughter was seriously injured in a road accident. Using the offices of then Minister of State for External Affairs R.L. Bhatia, Rabinder attempted to secure a posting to Washington, D.C. The request was turned down possibly because it was feared that this would make him available for recruitment by the CIA. After Rabinder's escape, a correspondent of the news magazine *Frontline* interviewed Bhatia. "My interest in the whole affair was purely compassionate," Bhatia told the correspondent. "Singh said he needed a lot of money to pay for his daughter's treatment, and that the Washington posting would help." However, Bhatia admitted that he made no effort to ascertain Rabinder Singh's integrity before pushing his case, relying only on pleas from two Amritsar businessmen.[1]

After his disappearance, many of his colleagues recalled that Rabinder had often expressed interest in the activities of others, with which he had little concern. There was also talk about him living a lavish lifestyle, and entertaining a lot. This appeared to be true. Once he had come to my office for a cup of tea, and asked me to tell him something about my sphere of work. In the Army, this was not only normal but considered desirable, and senior staff officers were expected to know what was happening in other branches of the organisation. I was dealing primarily with communications and the proposed VSAT network, on which I had recently given a presentation to the entire hierarchy. I told Rabinder that he could go through it if he wanted to refresh his memory. I could not tell him much about our resources for acquiring technical intelligence, since both terrestrial and satellite monitoring were being dealt with by the other joint secretaries, Verma and Yadav. I was dealing only with Internet monitoring, which was still in a formative stage, and we still had to make a start.

Subsequently, a newspaper reported that Rabinder's activities were first detected by a middle-rank officer in RAW's operations wing itself. S. Chandrashekhar - he later left the organisation to join the private sector - noticed that Rabinder had been asking for information outside his professional areas of concern. Chandrashekhar brought it to the notice of Amar Bhushan, the Special Secretary (Personnel), under whom the Counter Intelligence and Security (CIS) Division functioned. It was said that Rabinder was fed genuine but dated cipher traffic generated by the US mission in Islamabad which had been intercepted by one of our monitoring stations. The suspicions were confirmed when Rabinder promptly asked for more.

The newspapers reported that action against Rabinder had been recommended by RAW sometime in April, but was approved only on 14 May, which was also the day he disappeared. It was said that several reports on Rabinder had been sent to the National Security Adviser, Brajesh Misra, who was personally handling the case. Why it took the government almost a month to approve disciplinary action against Rabinder is a mystery, though there can be many reasons for it. The election results were about to be announced, and it was not certain if the NDA government would return to power. It is possible that the PMO felt that the thorny issue should be left to the new government to deal with. However, when the evidence against Rabinder mounted, the government had to act, and approved the recommendation of the RAW chief on 14 May 2004. The election results were announced immediately afterwards, and the NDA government was voted out.

On 05 June, the media reported the dismissal by the President of retired Major Rabinder Singh, under Article 311(2) (c) of the Constitution. This Article enables the President to dismiss any officer of an all-India service without holding a formal departmental enquiry against him if such an enquiry is considered not to be in the national interest. There is no provision for a judicial review of the decision. There were also reports that the government was considering approaching the US Government for his extradition. Considering the circumstances of the case, it is most unlikely that this will come through. Even if his whereabouts are known, the request can be refused in case Rabinder seeks's political asylum, which he certainly will.

Rabinder's escape left many questions unanswered. If he was indeed a mole, why was he allowed to get away? Why did RAW have to seek permission of the government to take action against him, once it was found that he was passing intelligence to a foreign agency? Surely, they could have had him arrested the day they came to know of his activities. Was he 'allowed' to get away, by people in RAW itself, who feared that they would be exposed if he was arrested and interrogated? Was Rabinder part of a larger network, which facilitated his escape? In the world of intelligence, spies are shown little mercy. If caught, their principals almost never acknowledge their existence. In normal circumstances, the Americans should have done the same thing, and denied that they had anything to do with Rabinder. The fact that they chose to whisk him out of India can only mean one thing – they did not want him to spill the beans about others like him, who were part of the network.

The defection of Rabinder exposed several shortcomings in the system. No intelligence agency in the world is immune to penetration. However, a good counter-intelligence mechanism is able to detect such penetrations well in time, so that the damage is minimal. Unfortunately, RAW did not have any counter-intelligence apparatus in place. Counter-intelligence came under the purview of the CIS Division, which also looked after physical security of the building, in addition to security of personnel and documents. When I joined, UK Katna was the Joint Secretary (Security). Under him was NK Sharma, who was the Director (Security). Katna reported to the Additional Secretary (Personnel). After Katna returned to the Delhi Police, no one was appointed to take over his job. The Joint Secretary (Personnel) began looking after the portfolio in addition to his duties. He was an extremely busy man, with most of his time being spent in mundane administrative matters, such as buildings, furnishings, allotment of accommodation, transport, posting and transfers, budgets, expenditure of funds, and a hundred other routine matters. As a result, the Director (Security) was virtually on his own, in matters concerning security.

NK Sharma was a police officer, whose primary concerns were access control mechanisms such as guards and sentries, boundary walls, steel gates, entry passes and so on. He had neither the training nor the acumen to deal with counter intelligence. As long as Katna was there, he kept Sharma on a tight leash. After Katna's departure, Sharma needed a hat that was several sizes larger. He developed a swagger and arrogance that would have done credit to Hitler's *Shutz Staffel*. On matters concerning security, Sharma began dealing with Amar Bhushan, who had assumed the title of Special Secretary (Personnel), even though he was the head of ARC.

It is said that Amar Bhushan had come to know of Rabinder's activities several months earlier, through S Chandrasekhar, and put him under surveillance. However, he did not inform Sahay about it until sometime in the middle of April. If Sahay had known about it earlier, perhaps he could have put some one more qualified on the case, instead of leaving it to the bumbling Sharma. RAW had several first class officers, with considerable experience in dealing with such matters. Perhaps he could have also sought the assistance of the IB, which reportedly has more expertise in the field, apart from a dedicated counter-intelligence team. It was only after this debacle, which almost cost Sahay his job that he told Amar Bhushan to stay away from RAW and confine himself to

Of course, the Rabinder episode was not the first such incident in RAW. In fact Rabinder's case was the third penetration of Indian Intelligence agencies by the CIA. The first known case was that of KV Unnikrishnan, the RAW Commissioner in Chennai who was convicted in 1987 for espionage. During his tenure in Colombo in 1981, he had become friendly with an American diplomat, and together with him, engaged in several extramarital affairs with unidentified women. After his return to India, he was briefly stationed at Delhi before moving to Chennai. Sometime in 1985, a woman describing herself as a stewardess with Pan American Airways telephoned him from Mumbai. She said that his American diplomat friend had told her to contact him in case she felt lonely. Unnikrishnan caught the next flight to Mumbai and spent some time with her in her hotel room. A liaison soon developed between the two, and in 1985-86, she gave him complimentary air tickets to accompany her on holidays to Singapore. During these jaunts in Singapore, the duo was photographed *in flagrante delicto*. The IB office in Chennai alerted RAW about Unnikrishnan's activities, and a joint surveillance and investigation team was set up. It was learned that he was working for the CIA, and passing copies of sensitive documents about RAW operations in Sri Lanka. In 1986, Unnikrishnan was arrested and spent a year in Tihar jail before being dismissed from service.[2] According to Raman, an ex-Additional Secretary in RAW, Prime Minister Rajiv Gandhi decided not to prosecute him, since he had already spent a year behind bars.

The Unnikrishnan case was a feather in the cap of the IB, and a slap on the face of RAW. However, the IB's smugness did not last long. In 1996, Rattan Sehgal was a contender for the top job in the IB. He had served for some time in the Ministry of External Affairs (MEA), where he was responsible for internal security and counter-intelligence. After his return to the IB from MEA, he was made the head of the counter-intelligence division. During his stint in the MEA, Sehgal had established contacts with several foreign intelligence operatives. He continued to maintain these links, without the knowledge of the Director IB. The IB's counter-intelligence division was keeping a tab on a woman CIA staffer in the US Embassy, who used a mobile phone to contact various people in the government. The IB's counter-intelligence team got a shock when they discovered that the mobile phone was registered in the name of their boss, Rattan Sehgal. This was brought to the notice of the Director IB, Arun Bhagat, who set up a joint team of RAW and IB to keep him under surveillance. The team was able to make a video recording of his meetings with the woman CIA officer, including footage of the time he had spent with her at a resort on the New Delhi-Jaipur highway. When confronted with this evidence, Sehgal admitted his contacts with her, and having given her a mobile phone to facilitate her operational work, which involved liaison with RAW on counter-terrorism and other matters. However, Sehgal denied having passed on any sensitive information. He was permitted to proceed on pre-mature retirement.[3]

Both Unnikrishnan and Sehgal had fallen prey to the 'honey-trap', which is one of the oldest techniques used by intelligence agencies to recruit spies. It is not known whether Rabinder had been inveigled by similar methods. However, the honey trap appears to be the favourite trick employed by the CIA, at least for Indians. In the latest case in 2006, a woman officer in the US Embassy, Rosanne Minchew, was found to be involved in a breach of security in the National Security Council Secretariat (NSCS). Commander Mukesh Saini was heading the National Information Security Coordination Cell in the NSCS. He was also the coordinator of the Indo-US Cyber Security Forum, and was in close contact with Minchew. They made several trips together, to Mumbai and Kolkata. Saini later resigned and joined an American company. But before he left, he had introduced Minchew to SS Paul, a computer analyst working under him at the NSCS. The Police already knew of Minchew's activities and were monitoring her mobile phone. They found a large number of SMSs from a particular number, which turned out to belong to Paul. Apparently, Paul passed on sensitive data on USB drives copied from the computers at the NSCS to Minchew, for which he was to be paid $ 50,000. It is feared that Paul may not the only beneficiary of the CIA's largesse.[4]

Along with Saini and Paul, a senior RAW officer also came under a cloud. He was Brigadier Ujjal Dasgupta, the Director (Computers) in RAW, an appointment he had been holding for the last six years. On 16 June 2006, newspapers reported that his office was searched and sealed by a team of officials from both IB and RAW. Dasgupta was asked not to come to the office, and to stay at home until his case is decided. Though he was not detained, he was subjected to sustained questioning by the officials of IB and RAW. Investigators could not find any concrete evidence of him leaking national secrets to any foreign agency. However, it was found that he was in contact with foreign nationals, about whom he should have informed the headquarters, but failed to do so. The case came to light after the IB routinely checked back with RAW headquarters if the officer was authorised to maintain foreign contacts. Dasgupta was subsequently arrested after more evidence of his involvement came to light. During his police custody, he revealed that he had thrown some pen drives in a well in Nehru Park, very close to the place where he lived. The pen drives were recovered, and found to contain sensitive data that should not have left his office.

Rabinder's case is important for several reasons. Unlike most of the other moles who were caught, Rabinder managed to escape. In almost all other cases, the extent of damage was known, since the persons concerned were either caught with the documents or revealed what they had passed on during interrogation. In Rabinder's case, literally nothing is known. The government has not revealed the quantity and type of information that he had passed on to the CIA. It was also not known for how long he had been doing this. It is mind boggling to think that he could have been at it for ten years, or even more! At the time of his escape, the government came out with the statement that it is unlikely that he had revealed any sensitive information, since he was handling the South East Asia desk. Apart from the implied affront to the countries in the region, the statement strains the credulity of everyone. If it is indeed true that RAW has joint secretaries who do little more than push files, it does little credit to the organisation. In fact, this corroborates the view in many quarters that RAW is overstaffed and could do with some reduction in size. Most important, if Rabinder has not revealed anything, what is the big hue and cry about? Suppose he resurfaces one day, saying that he had met with an accident and lost his memory or was in a coma, like it happens so often in Bollywood films and popular soaps on TV? Will he get back his job in RAW? Unless the government comes up with some hard evidence against him – so far it hasn't – this may well happen.

End Notes

1.   *Frontline,* 02 July 2004.

2.   *The Sunday Hindustan Times,* 09 July 2006. p.10.

3.   ibid.

4.   ibid.

11

The Intelligence Mechanism in India

Having seen the functioning of RAW from close quarters, I was able to form an opinion about its internal strengths and weaknesses. I also witnessed the changes in the intelligence set up in the country, especially after the Kargil operations. There is no doubt that RAW has been at the receiving end in several articles highlighting the intelligence failures in recent years, with rarely a word of praise for its achievements. This is indeed unfortunate and unfair, but unavoidable, given the environmental constraints under which the agency functions. It is important to remember that RAW has no control over many external factors that have a direct bearing over its performance. Among the most important of these are inter-agency rivalry, ambiguity about its role and responsibilities vis-à-vis the IB and MI, lack of accountability and the absence of a suitable supervisory mechanism.

The rivalry between the three major intelligence agencies– RAW, IB and MI – has done incalculable damage not only to the agencies themselves but also the nation. Some of the reasons for this professional jealousy are historical. During the

Nehru years, IB had a virtual monopoly over the entire spectrum of intelligence, internal and external, civil and military. The hegemony ended with the creation of RAW in 1968, when the external intelligence division of IB and the Director General Security (DGS), along with the ARC and its TECHINT resources were transferred to RAW. The intelligence failures in 1962 and 1965 stung the Army leading to the strengthening of its HUMINT capability and the establishment of its own SIGINT facility in the form of the Directorate of Signals Intelligence. With the passage of time, the situation has only worsened, and apart from these three major players, several others have joined the race. Today, almost every para-military and police force has its own intelligence network.

The rivalry between intelligence agencies is often taken to ridiculous limits. Soon after I joined RAW, I visited Srinagar. Atop the Shankaracharya hill, I counted almost a dozen antennae, each belonging to a different intelligence agency or para military force. All of them were intercepting the same radio transmissions from across the border or from terrorist groups based in India. In most cases, the intercepts were finally going to the same consumer. However, let alone sharing the information, none of the personnel even talked to each other. What a waste of resources, I thought. At another location in Jammu and Kashmir, I found that the RAW monitoring station was located right next to a wireless experimental unit of the Army. One of the aerial masts of our station was askew, because a guy rope had snapped, and they did not have a spare. When I told our men to borrow one from the Army detachment, they were aghast. "We do not enter their enclosure", they said, "and neither do we allow them to enter ours".

Once, I accompanied the Chief Military Intelligence Adviser (CMIA), Major General PK Puri, to call on Major General AS Bhagat, who had just taken over as Additional Director General, Signals Intelligence. 'Andy' Bhagat was a fine officer, and an old friend. (Shortly afterwards, he was afflicted with cancer and suffered a premature death). We discussed with him the possibility of sharing at least technical intelligence, such as the equipment, frequencies and call signs being used by our target countries. Bhagat agreed immediately. After I returned to our office I discussed the matter with the Adviser (Tele) and other officers in the Telecom Division. I was surprised to find that the idea had no takers.

It is believed that about 85 percent of the output of ARC and about 25 percent of what is produced by RAW goes to the Armed Forces.[1] When RAW was created, it had only two officers of the rank of joint secretary, one of them being the CMIA, who was a serving major general. Today, RAW has more than a dozen special secretaries and additional secretaries who outrank the CMIA. This is an indication of the gradual erosion in the importance of military intelligence in RAW, which pays greater attention to political intelligence of neighbouring as well as distant countries. Military authorities argue, not without justification, that political intelligence about American, European and Asian nations, with the exception of India's immediate neighbours, is of little relevance to the consumers. In any case, 90 percent of such intelligence comes from open sources, such as the Internet and the local media. On the other hand, the amount of military intelligence that can be gleaned from open sources is miniscule. Should not RAW be directing a substantial portion of its resources on gathering military intelligence?

One of the severest indictments of RAW came from the Kargil Review Committee, which noted:"....the primary responsibility for collecting external intelligence, including that relating to a potential adversary's military deployment, is vested in RAW. The DGMI's capability for intelligence collection is limited. .... Therefore, it is primarily RAW, which must provide intelligence about a likely attack, whether across a broad or narrow front. Unfortunately, the RAW facility in the Kargil area did not receive adequate attention in terms of staff or technological capability. The station was under Srinagar, but reported to Leh, which was not focused on Kargil but elsewhere. Hence intelligence collection, coordination and follow-up were weak."

Of course, RAW counters the accusation by claiming that it is accountable for only strategic and not tactical military intelligence, which is the responsibility of the intelligence directorates of the Armed Forces. RAW officers also complain that the Army always blames intelligence agencies when it's operations fail, but rarely gives credit when they succeed. However, this accusation appears to be ungracious. After its spectacular victory against East Pakistan in 1971, the Army commended the contribution of RAW, leading Prime Minister Indira Gandhi to remark: "RAW officers should not allow this praise to go to their head. The Army is generous in praising the RAW because it won the war."[2]

The Kargil Review Committee did not absolve the Army of blame altogether, observing: "The Indian Army did not share information about the intensity and effect of its past firing with others. In the absence of this information, RAW could not correctly assess the significance of enemy activity in terms of ammunition storage or construction of underground bunkers...The Army never shared its intelligence with the other agencies or with the JIC. There was no system of Army authorities at different levels from the DGMI downwards providing feedback to the agencies."

The Army justifies its failure to share tactical intelligence with other because of practical reasons. Being the end-user of military intelligence, it feels that it is of not much use to anyone else. Considering the thousands of points from where such intelligence emanates, it would be an impossible task to collate and disseminate it to other agencies in time to be of any use to them. A large portion of such intelligence is of interest only to neighbouring units and formations and is rarely sent right up the chain of command. It would require a colossal amount of effort to collect all the inputs at Delhi or even the command headquarters, from where they can be passed on to other agencies. In most cases, follow up action on the intelligence is completed before it reaches higher headquarters, making it redundant.

The reluctance to share intelligence is the bane of all agencies, at least in India. Ideally, tactical military intelligence collected by any agency should be shared immediately with the local formation headquarters, enabling it to act on it immediately. This rarely happens, because the agency gets no credit for it. The heads of the concerned agencies prefer to see the intelligence themselves before passing it on to the end user, so that in case it results in a major success, they are not denied credit for it. This proclivity to earn acclaim has given rise to the unpardonable trend in every agency of keeping vital intelligence close to its chest, until it is disclosed to someone important enough in the political hierarchy, sometimes the Prime Minister himself. In some cases, such intelligence is even made public, in an effort to discredit another country, in violation of the basic principles of intelligence.

A glaring example of this trend was the famous telephone conversation between General Pervez Musharraf and his Chief of Staff, Lieutenant General Mohammed Aziz, which was broadcast on radio and TV before the whole world to prove Pakistan's complicity in the Kargil war. It is not known how many brownie points India earned with the United States or the United Nations. What is certain is that Pakistan came to know that the particular satellite link between Beijing and Islamabad was being intercepted by RAW, leading to its immediate closure. It is impossible to estimate the value of intelligence that would have been obtained, if the link had continued to be used.

Perhaps no one in RAW or the PMO had read FW Winterbotham's *Ultra Secret* or Peter Calvocoressi's *Top Secret Ultra,* both published in 1974, which revealed for the first time details of an important source of intelligence during World

War II. Very early in the war, Britain had broken the code being used on Enigma, the enciphering device being used by the Germans. This information was zealously protected and the Germans continued using Enigma throughout the war, yielding a rich harvest to British intelligence. In several instances, British lives were lost, since saving them would have revealed to the Germans the source of the intelligence, resulting in its drying up. In one instance, an intercept revealed that the *Luftwaffe* was going to bomb Coventry the next morning. The town could have been evacuated, and the lives of its residents saved. Churchill took the agonising decision not to do so, since it would have resulted in the discontinuance of the use of Enigma by the Germans. It is futile to expect such mettle in our own political leaders, who not only agreed to release three dreaded terrorists after the hijacking of IC 814 but also sent a cabinet minister to escort them to Kandahar.

The rivalry between the IB and RAW is well known and perhaps unavoidable, in view of their past history and functions. Though the IB is tasked with internal intelligence, it is also responsible for counter intelligence, which frequently concerns personnel serving in other intelligence agencies such as RAW as well as the staff of foreign missions in India. This frequently brings it in conflict with the MEA and RAW. Cross border terrorism, *hawala* transactions and smuggling of arms and narcotics are areas that concern both IB and RAW, with each unwilling to let go of its jurisdiction. In fact, it is difficult to differentiate between internal and external intelligence in today's environment, with borders being blurred or obliterated by satellite phones, Internet and air travel. An Indian recruited by a foreign militant group is definitely the concern of the IB. When he is taken across the border for training he becomes the interest of RAW. When he re-enters India and carries out strikes against military installations in Jammu and Kashmir it becomes the worry of MI. Should he be handed over from one agency to the other every time he crosses a border, or should all keep a watch on him together? Should the Army and IB be allowed to monitor trans-border radio and satellite links, which strictly fall within the purview of RAW? Should RAW have the authority to monitor telephone calls and e-mails originating or terminating in India, if the other party is based in a foreign country? These are questions that have no clear answers, and only add to the blame game between the intelligence agencies.

Other than the IB and MI, another organisation with which RAW has always had a love-hate relationship is the Ministry of External Affairs (MEA). One of the important tasks assigned to RAW is the collection of intelligence in foreign countries. The types of intelligence may be political, military, economic, scientific or technological. Of these, political intelligence is considered the most vital, except for China and Pakistan where military intelligence is equally important. The political intelligence collected by RAW forms an important input in deciding the nation's foreign policy, whose implementation is the primary responsibility of the MEA. It would appear that the MEA, as the major consumer of RAW's output, would be more than favourably inclined towards the latter. Unfortunately, this does not happen, at least at the functional level.

Since the MEA and the heads of missions in foreign capitals are the end users, it is imperative that they are involved in deciding the intelligence tasks given to RAW and their priorities. Ideally, they should also monitor the implementation of these tasks and evaluate the inputs given to them by RAW, with a view to refine and optimize them. It was with this in mind that the post of a Foreign Service Adviser was created in RAW when it was first formed. The post was to be held by a senior officer of the Indian Foreign Service, who could act as a link between the MEA and RAW and assist in the implementation of political intelligence tasks assigned to the latter, as well as evaluation of its output. Due to some reason, the system has fallen into disuse.

RAW officers are deputed to foreign missions in cover appointments to carry out the task of collecting political intelligence. In some cases, technical personnel of RAW are also deputed to man. communications and gather SIGINT at selected locations. RAW personnel often complain that they are not treated well by the Foreign Service officers, who consider them 'freeloaders', enjoying diplomatic privileges and perquisites without earning their keep. The MEA's major grouse is that RAW operatives in the missions keep information from them, preferring to send it to their own headquarters. By the time the intelligence reaches the MEA in Delhi and back to the mission through diplomatic channels, it is usually outdated. Even when the intelligence is shared, it is found to have been collected mostly from open sources, and is of little value.

During the last decade, the country's security and intelligence apparatus has been restructured. The National Security Council (NSC) took over the functions of the Joint Intelligence Council in 1998. After the Kargil conflict, the Defence Intelligence Agency (DIA) and the National Technical Resources Organisation (NTRO) came into being. However, the exact functions and boundaries of these agencies are still not clear. The DIA is now the nodal agency for all defence related intelligence, with control over the Directorate of Signals Intelligence as well as the Defence Image Processing and Analysis Centre (DIPAC). What happens to RAW? Should it continue collecting military intelligence? If not, should it not wind up the office of the CMIA and withdraw or transfer its assets that are deployed in border regions and in foreign countries for collecting military intelligence? A similar situation exists in NTRO, which was designed to bring all technical resources for collecting intelligence under one roof. However, the ARC refused to part with its assets and continues doing what it has been doing earlier. The reluctance is understandable – ARC aircraft come in handy for trips by the top brass of RAW and their families. It was an ARC aircraft that ferried Admiral Sushil Kumar from Cochin to Delhi when Admiral Vishnu Bhagwat was sacked. As C-in-C Southern Naval

Command, Kumar was authorised to travel in an IAF aircraft of the Communication Squadron, yet he elected to use the ARC aircraft. Perhaps it was feared that Air Headquarters would refuse the IAF aircraft, unless it received an official request in accordance with the rules. If nothing else, the Air Chief would have informed Bhagwat, who could have forestalled the move.

The only other agency with substantial technical assets is the Army, which naturally will not give anything to the NTRO since the DIA is now responsible for military intelligence. Where does this leave the NTRO? Of course, it can acquire new assets, but this will take another 5-10 years. Even then, it is unlikely to end the rivalry between the agencies or the duplication of resources, which was the reason for its creation in the first place. All that the NTRO will achieve is the creation of several hundred new posts and a colossal waste of public money. As far as intelligence is concerned, it is difficult to see how it will enhance our capabilty.

A point that is frequently debated is the lack of accountability and obsession with secrecy of intelligence agencies in India. In a break with tradition, RAW recently invited an 'outsider' to its precincts to deliver a lecture. The occasion was the first RN Kao memorial lecture that was held on 20 January 2007 in the RAW auditorium. The subject of the lecture was 'India and Global Security: Leveraging Soft Power', and the speaker was Shashi Tharoor, Under Secretary General for Communications and Public Information, at the United Nations. A well-known author and diplomat, Tharoor had thrown his hat in the ring for the post of Secretary General, to succeed Kofi Annan in December 2006. However, he pulled out of the race when it became clear that he did not have the support of the majority of Asian countries, which favoured Ban Ki-moon of the Republic of Korea, who finally got the job.

In the presence of a galaxy of the intelligence community that included the Cabinet Secretary, the National Security

Adviser and several ex-chiefs of RAW, Tharoor highlighted the irrelevance of the obsessive secrecy that envelopes RAW and its activities. He felt that the facelessness of RAW may be working to its disadvantage, since its personnel were not getting the recognition they deserved for their valuable contribution to India's foreign policy. Noting that the agency was not accountable to Parliament and its funds were subject to only a limited scrutiny, Tharoor argued that RAW was being distrusted and criticised by the media and the public, without it having any chance to defend its actions. . "RAW's exact locus within the Indian strategic establishment has remained a puzzle", he said. He also commented on the lack of clarity in the role of RAW, which led other intelligence and security institutions, including the police and the army to disregard RAW's expertise in counter-terrorism, treating it as meddling in issues of internal security. Tharoor went on to add: "I think it is a great pity if it is true that, as I am told, secrecy has gone to the point where many who serve in RAW themselves do not have a sense of their own history."[3]

The need for accountability and parliamentary oversight is accepted by several officers who were once part of RAW, including B. Raman, an ex Additional Secretary. According to him, "India is amongst the countries. ...which continue to follow the dictum that the intelligence agencies are the most patriotic, can do wrong and hence don't need external checks and balances. There is no desire on the part of the political leadership to make the agencies accountable for their performance."[4]

It is relevant to note that most democracies have put in place systems for external checks on their intelligence agencies. In the USA, the Senate Select Committee on Intelligence and the House of Representatives Permanent Select Committee on Intelligence exercise parliamentary oversight over the CIA.. These committees receive all intelligence output of the CIA, which also conducts regular briefings for the members and their staff. The CIA also has a system of internal oversight in the form of the Inspector General (IG, CIA) who carries out inspections, audit and enquiries in respect of intelligence failures and misdemeanours. Though he works under the Director Central Intelligence, the IG, CIA is appointed by the President and is not subject to congressional oversight. In addition to the above, oversight is also exercised by the President's Foreign Intelligence Advisory Board, which comprises trustworthy and eminent citizens with experience whose job is to see that intelligence agencies do not violate laws of the land or indulge in unethical practices.

In the UK, oversight is exercised by the parliamentary Intelligence and Security Committee (ISC) that is appointed by and reports to the Prime Minister. The staff support for the committee is provided by the Cabinet Office, which is similar to India's Cabinet Secretariat. In a sense, the ISC is not a parliamentary committee but a committee of parliamentarians, functioning under the Executive instead of the British Parliament. Canada has a Security Intelligence Review Committee (SIRC) that consists of five Privy Councillors who are appointed for five years. The SIRC oversees the functioning of the Canadian Security Intelligence Service (CSIS) and reports to the Canadian House of Commons. In addition, there is an IG, CSIS who carries out functions similar those of the IG, CIA in the USA.[5]

In Australia, the Parliamentary Joint Committee on the Australian Intelligence exercises oversight over the Australian Security Intelligence Organisation (ASIO), the Australian Secret Intelligence Service (ASIS) as well as the Defence Signals Directorate (DSD). In addition, oversight is exercised by the Office of National Assessments (ONA) and the Inspector General of Intelligence and Security (IGIS). New Zealand has three tiers of supervision, in the form of the Cabinet Strategy Subcommittee on Intelligence and Security, chaired by the Prime Minister, the Intelligence and Security Committee and the Inspector-General of Intelligence and Security (IGIS). These oversee the functioning of New Zealand's two intelligence agencies, the New Zealand Security Intelligence Service (NZSIS) and the Government Communications Security Bureau (GCSB).

As can be seen, almost all democracies have some form of parliamentary oversight over their intelligence agencies. India has the dubious distinction of being the lone exception, in spite of having one of the oldest intelligence agencies in the world. The demand for such over sight has often been made in various forums, with little effect. Almost thirty years ago, the Shah Commission was set up to enquire into the Emergency imposed by Indira Gandhi in 1975. Commenting on the need for external control, it noted: "...for the effective and objective functioning of the intelligence agencies, their activities and achievements should be suitably overseen, and evaluated by responsible forums functioning independently of the intelligence agencies."[6]

The only attempt to introduce an oversight mechanism was made during the tenure of Prime Minister VP Singh. The suggestion for parliamentary oversight had reportedly come from Jaswant Singh, who was then Chairman of the Estimates Committee of the Lok Sabha. The Secretary (R) convened a meeting of senior officers in RAW to seek their views on the proposed measure. To his pleasant surprise, most of the officers came out strongly in favour of it, as they felt that this would make them less vulnerable to undesirable pressures from the executive. Interaction with Members of Parliament would also give them a chance to acquaint parliamentarians and through them the public with the work being done by the intelligence agencies. This would in turn remove the wrong impressions that most of them carried in their minds about intelligence agencies. Unfortunately, before the exercise could be completed the VP Singh government fell due to withdrawal of support by the BJP.[7]

The need for a mechanism for external evaluation of the performance of intelligence agencies cannot be denied.

Presently, this function is carried out by the National Security Council Secretariat (NSCS). However, the NSCS is constituted by and reports to the Executive. It cannot replace a Committee of Parliament, which is the highest forum of accountability for all organs of the government. The fear of breach of security is misplaced, and illogical. In a multi-party democracy like India, any party can form a government. The Prime Minister as well as his colleagues who look after important portfolios such as Defence, Home and Foreign Affairs can be from any party. It is downright foolish to suggest that they can be trusted with sensitive information only when they are occupying berths in the Union Cabinet, and become untrustworthy when they are in the Opposition. It is nobody's case that the entire Parliament should have access to sensitive information. But there is definitely no harm in forming a select committee, whose members can be nominated by the Prime Minister in consultation with the Leader of Opposition. Regular briefings by heads of intelligence agencies will have many advantages. The Prime Minister will have the benefit of impartial advice about the performance of the agencies from the parliamentary committee. When there is a change in government, the new incumbents whose portfolios have something to do with intelligence will not be at sea, as at present - there is a good chance of some of the new ministers having served on the parliamentary committee dealing with intelligence while sitting in the Opposition. The intelligence agencies will also benefit, since they will have a forum to refute false allegations against them. It is high time that the representatives of the people exercise their right of knowing how our intelligence agencies function, and whether the taxpayers money is being properly spent. They owe it to the people who elected them. India cannot continue with a democratic form of government with the intelligence set up of a totalitarian state.

Endnotes

1. B. Raman, *Intelligence: Past, Present and Future*, p.71

2. Ibid, p. 72

3. *The Indian·Express*, New Delhi, 21 January 2007

4. B. Raman, p.11

5. Ibid, pp. 364-377

6. Bhasyam Kasturi, *Intelligence Services: Analysis, Organisation and Function*, p.79, quoting Shah Commission of Inquiry Interim Report II, p.146.

7. B. Raman, p. 80

12

Epilogue

Intelligence is often called the second oldest profession, yielding place to one that is the exclusive preserve of the fairer sex. From the earliest times, kings realized that military might alone was not enough to protect their kingdoms – spies were a necessary adjunct to their troops. Chanankya's *Arthashastra* remains one of the most authoritative texts on the subject, having guided Indian rulers for over 2500 years. Statecraft and governance depend on many instruments to extend their power and achieve their objectives, the most visible being military power and diplomacy. However, without intelligence, the other tools of governance lose their cutting edge. Intelligence and security are two faces of the same coin, and one cannot exist without the other.

Intelligence and security agencies exist in all nations. However, they suffer from a peculiar disease. After some time, they become so big that they often devour their creator. This phenomenon occurs more often in totalitarian regimes or military dictatorships than in democracies, where the other organs of the state - the legislature and the judiciary - and the fourth estate act as a check on the executive. Without this system of checks and balances, there is a real danger of intelligence and security agencies becoming a law unto themselves. The ISI in Pakistan is an excellent example of this phenomenon. In most developed nations, intelligence and security agencies operate within boundaries defined by law. One would expect a similar situation to prevail in India, given its rich cultural heritage, democratic traditions and a vibrant economy. This, unfortunately, is not true. The world's largest democracy appears to have little control over its intelligence apparatus.

Intelligence agencies in India strongly object to any form of parliamentary supervision, whenever the subject is discussed. This is only to be expected, considering that it would expose the chinks in their armour. The government of the day is reluctant to introduce any form of parliamentary control, fearing that it would dilute their own authority, and prevent them from using the services of these agencies to spy on their political opponents. Not surprisingly, political parties raise a hue and cry about their telephones being tapped as long as they are sitting on the Opposition benches. The moment they move to the Treasury benches, they have a lapse of memory, and forget about these incidents. The dozens of human rights groups that vociferously protest against violation of rights such as the right to education, the right to equality and the right to religion remain silent on the issue of the most important right of all – the right to privacy. Ironically, the intelligence agencies that violate the citizen's right to privacy are funded from taxes collected from him. It is a classic case of the dog biting the hand that feeds him.

Intelligence is a tool, or an input that is required by the country's policy makers and planners to further her global and regional interests. A career diplomat is not always the best person to decide the nation's foreign policy, and neither is an economist best suited to formulate economic policies. Then why should we leave it to the heads of IB and RAW to decide on the intelligence needs of the nation? Should not the people's representatives, sitting in Parliament, have a say in

Intelligence is not the only 'holy cow' that nobody wants to touch. Another bogey is security, which is often touted by security agencies and the government to avoid answering uncomfortable questions about their failings in this sphere. After the 1962 debacle, the Chief of Army Staff ordered an enquiry to go into the lapses that led to the disaster. The NEFA Enquiry, as it came to be known, was conducted by Lieutenant General Henderson Brooks and Brigadier PS Bhagat, VC. The Enquiry Report was submitted to the Army Chief, General JN Chaudhury on 12 May 1963, and he in turn forwarded it to the Defence Minister, YB Chavan, on 2 July 1963. Instead of placing it before Parliament, the Government promptly declared it Top Secret, and kept the copy under its own custody, even though the Army and not the Government of India ordered it. This happened when Nehru, known for his respect for democratic values, was the Prime Minister of India. Though the Indian Parliament did not get to see the report, a foreign correspondent, Neville Maxwell, was somehow able to read it, and he has written about it in his book *'India's-China War'*.

After the Kargil intrusions in 1999, the Government constituted the Kargil Review Committee to go into the intelligence failures that contributed to the fiasco. When the report was placed before Parliament, about 15 pages dealing with intelligence were removed, on grounds of security. Not one of the honourable members sitting in the House questioned the implied insult and aspersion on their integrity. Can there be a greater breach of privilege than this? Yet, nobody thought it fit to raise the issue on the floor of the house. If the Group of Ministers could see the report, why not the honourable members of Parliament? Those who held important portfolios of Defence, Home and Finance at that time are today sitting in the Opposition. And those from whom the report was intended to be kept are today in the Government. So, members of both sides have seen it. Does it still make sense to keep it away from Parliament?

After the assassination of Indira Gandhi, the SPG was raised to protect the Prime Minister. Like the Secret Service in the USA, the SPG is expected to protect the life of the Chief Executive. However, it was never intended that this should be done by causing hardship to the general public. Roads are closed for long periods, leading to traffic jams. People miss flights and trains, and seriously ill patients cannot reach the hospital in time. Often, the airport itself is closed, and flights are diverted to other stations, causing great inconvenience to everyone. The SPG treats common citizens like cattle, and we put up with it! Why should we? Is the life of one person more important than that of the critically ill patient being rushed to hospital? Surely there are better methods of providing proximate security than by closing roads and airports.

When Jimmy Carter was President of the USA, his cavalcade went through a red light at a road junction. A teenager, who was coming from another road, hit the President's limousine. The Secret Service agents travelling with the President immediately pounced on the hapless youngster, and hauled him to the police station. He was let off when it was found that he had no ulterior motives. However, the youngster refused to go. He felt that he had done nothing wrong, since the light was green for him. It was the President who was at fault, driving through a red light. He insisted on an apology from the President himself. The President of the USA had to apologise to the teenager, for violating the law, and driving through a red light. Contrast this with the behaviour of the SPG when three youngsters drove up to the Prime Minister's house, wanting to meet him. When they were told that they could not meet him, they turned around and drove off. But the SPG suddenly discovered that they should not have driven past the first gate, and entered a high security area. A message was flashed on the wireless, the trio was intercepted and arrested, and the car was impounded. Of course, no body bothered to ask the SPG what crime had been committed, and why they had been permitted to enter the high security zone in the first instance.

Today, almost all important public buildings in the capital have been closed to the general public. This includes the Rashtrapati Bhawan, Parliament House, South and North Blocks, Vigyan Bhawan and several others. At one stage, even India Gate was closed to the public after a perceived security threat. Even today, anyone can drive, bicycle or jog in front of the White House in Washington DC. After the bombings of the World Trade Centre in New York on September 11, the security agencies in the USA proposed that Capitol Hill should be closed to the public. There was an uproar, and people argued that the Capitol belongs to the American people and not the senators and congressmen who sit there. The proposal was dropped. Why should the Indian citizen be treated differently? Must we surrender our rights and privileges to the whims of security personnel, who impose such restrictions only to cover up their own deficiencies?

The two premier intelligence agencies in India are the IB and RAW, looking after internal and external intelligence respectively. Both function more or less independently, without any curbs or supervision. Coming under the Ministry of Home affairs, the IB has a modicum of ministerial control. RAW does not even have this fig leaf of restraint to curb its activities. There is no doubt that RAW and IB, like intelligence agencies anywhere else, must work under the direct control of Executive. The same is true for other organs such as the Armed Forces, which are tasked with safeguarding the nation's borders and the lives of its citizens. But the Chiefs of the three Services do not decide when to go to war, or which country to attack? This is the prerogative of the Government, which is in turn answerable to the people, through Parliament. Is it not strange that our intelligence agencies are exempted from such controls, which even the Armed Forces are subservient to? If war is too serious a business to be left to generals, should not intelligence be considered too serious a business to be left to spies?

Bibliography

Books

Abedin, Zainul. *RAW and Bangla Desh*. Dhaka: Madina Publications, 1995

Ashraf, Fahmida.. *RAW: Covert Instrument of Indian Ambitions*. Islamabad: Institute of Strategic Studies, October 2004.

Cohen, Stephen P. *India: Emerging Power*. New Delhi: Oxford University Press, 2003.

Dhar, M.K. *Open Secrets – India's Intelligence Unveiled*. New Delhi: Manas Publications, 2005

Kapur, Harish. *Diplomacy in India: Then and Now*. New Delhi: Manas Publications, 2002.

Kasturi, Dr Bhashyam. *Intelligence Services: Analysis, Organisation and Function*. New Delhi, Lancer Publishers & Distributors, 1995

Krishna, R.G. *India: A Nation in Turmoil*. New Delhi: UBS Publishers & Distributors, 2001.

Pathak, D.C. *Intelligence; A Security Weapon*. New Delhi: Manas Publications, 2003.

Raina, Ashok. *Inside RAW: The Story of India's Secret Service*. New Delhi: Vikas Publishing House, 1981.

Raman, B. *Intelligence: Past, Present and Future.* New Delhi: Lancer Publishers & Distributors, 2002.

Sagar, Tariq Ismail. *RAW: Research and Analysis Wing.* Lahore: Sagar Publishers.

Singh, Major General V.K. *Leadership in the Indian Army: Biographies of Twelve Soldiers.* New Delhi: Sage Publications, 2005.

Tirmazi, Brigadier Syed A.I. *Profiles of Intelligence.* Lahore: Fiction House, 1995.

Articles

Aslam Khan, 'US report details direct RAW involvement in East Pakistan secession', *Pakistan Defence Journal*, February 2000.

Hali, Group Captain S.M. 'RAW at War : Genesis of Secret Agencies in Ancient India'. *Pakistan Defence Journal*, February-March, 1999.

Kasturi, Dr Bhashyam, 'Military Intelligence in India: An Analysis'. *The Indian Defence Review, 1997*

Lodi, Lieutenant General FS. 'RAW and Bangladesh'. *Pakistan Defence Journal*, February 2000.

Lodi, Lieutenant General FS. 'Is India a terrorist state?' *Pakistan Defence Journal*, May 2000.

Mazari, Dr. Shireen M. 'RAW facts on South Asia'. *Pakistan Defence Journal*, January 1999.

Nayar, Kuldip. 'Spies: Myth and Reality.' *The Tribune*, 14 July, 1983.

Raman, B. 'On the RAW Hunt'. *Observer Research Foundation*, 2005.

Swami, Praveen. 'A New Intelligence Organisation'. *Frontline*, Vol.19, Issue 06, 16-29 March, 2002.

Index